U0920059

FULFILLING DREAMS OF NEW CAMPUS
BEGINNING A NEW 60-YEAR CIRCLE

Planning and Construction Memoir of the Peiyang Garden Campus of Tianjin University

圆梦新校区 启航新甲子

天津大学北洋园校区规划建设实录

本书编委会 著

圆梦新校区
启航新甲子

庆祝天津大学新校区建设
第一期工程完工

吴咏诗书 二〇一五年九月

本书编委会 Editorial Committee of the Book

序一

巍巍学府，北洋天大，作为我国近代高等教育史上建校最早的高等学府，2015年10月2日，天津大学（北洋大学）将迎来120年双甲子校庆纪念日，届时，天津大学北洋园校区也将全面投入使用，开启下一个甲子学校发展的蓝图与规划。

天津大学（前身北洋大学）于1895年10月2日由光绪皇帝钦准设立，1951年定名为天津大学，是1959年中共中央首批确定的16所全国重点大学之一，也是“211工程”“985工程”首批重点建设的大学。如今的天津大学形成了以工为主、理工结合，经、管、文、法、教育等多学科协调发展的学科布局。

从海河之畔的梁家园博文书院到花堤蔼蔼的西沽，从艰苦卓绝的七星灯火到快速发展的卫津路校园，天大校舍的每一次变迁都推动着学校不断发展。天津大学北洋园校区建设是学校事业发展历史上的重大机遇，关系到学校当前和长远发展，关系到师生员工的切身利益。我校于2009年底启动了北洋园新校区筹建工作，2015年9月新校区投入使用。新校区按照世界一流大学的标准谋划布局，为学校内涵式发展、进一步提高办学质量提供了支撑和保障。

新校区的规划建设得到了教育部、天津市委市政府的高度重视和大力支持，市领导多次听取和研究我校新校区规划设计汇报，并作出重要指示。为了高水平、高质量做好新校区的总体规划，天津大学邀请聘用了一批国内外知名建筑规划大师、杰出校友组成专家工作营，同时，开放地聘请国内外知名专家学者组成专家咨询组，全程以工作营的方式参与规划。在新校区的建设中坚持高起点规划、高水平设计、高标准管理。我们力求使北洋园校区反映天津大学百年的历史文化，传承文明、传承传统；反映天津大学未来发展的水平和标准，符合建设世界一流大学的办学目标；反映当代国内外建筑领域的先进水平；也反映天津大学广大师生和历届校友的共同愿望。

天津大学作为一所百年老校，在其办学的历程中为国家培养了20万余名社会精英，他们是天津大学事业发展的重要依靠力量。天津大学北洋园新校区的建设，始终在各地校友的关注和支持下进行，海内外校友也纷纷捐赠，以各种形式助力新校区发展。新校区的一草一木都凝聚着全体北洋人、天大人的智慧和力量。天大的未来不仅是我们的未来，更是广大校友们的共同期盼，愿校友们的情感之花在新校区的土地上持久绽放。

“圆梦新校区，启航新甲子”，是圆天大兴学强国之梦、严谨治学之梦、爱国奉献之梦。天津大学北洋园校区的建设投用，是天津大学一个重要的里程碑，是天津大学事业腾飞的崭新起点，也是我们全体天大人奋发图强的新起点。抓住搬迁新校区的机遇，坚持走天津大学特色的内涵发展之路，不断提升学校综合实力，为把我校早日建成世界知名高水平大学，进而建成世界一流大学而努力奋斗。

在此，对关心和支持天津大学新校区建设的各界人士、全体师生、广大校友以及为新校区建设辛勤奋战的一线同志们表示最诚挚的谢意。

刘建平

2015年8月

Preface 1

As the earliest institution of higher education in modern Chinese higher education history, Tianjin University (Peiyang University) will welcome its 120th anniversary on October 2nd, 2015. At the appointed time, Peiyang Garden Campus of Tianjin University will be put into use completely, to start the next 60-year blueprint and plan for university development.

Establishment of Tianjin University (former Peiyang University) was approved by Guangxu Emperor on October 2nd, 1895. It is renamed as Tianjin University in 1951, one of 16 national key universities defined by the Central Committee of the Communist Party of China, and a key construction unit of "211 Project" and "985 Project". Tianjin University has formed the discipline layout of giving priority to engineering, combining science and engineering, and developing economics, management, arts, laws, and education harmoniously.

From Liangjia Garden Bowen Academy along the Haihe River to Xigu with flowers, and from arduous 7-star Light to rapidly developed Weijin Road Campus, each change of Tianjin University has promoted continuous development. The construction of Peiyang Garden New Campus is an important opportunity in the university' s development cause, invoving the university' s current and long-term development and immediate interests of teachers and students. The new campus started planning in the end of 2009 and it will be put into use in September, 2015. The new campus is planed as per standard of world-class universities, providing support and guarantee for the university' s connotative development and quality promotion of school running.

The planning and construction of the new campus is highly concerned and strongly supported by the Ministry of Education and Tianjin Municipal Party Committee and Government. Municipal leaders have listened and researched the new campus' planning and design report for many times and given important indicators. In order to complete the new campus' overall planning with high level and high quality, a batch of famous master architects in construction planning at home and abroad and outstanding alumni were invited to form the work camp . And at the same time, many famous experts and scholars at home and abroad were invited to form the expert consultation group. High-starting-point plan, high-level design, and high-standard management are insisted in the construction of the new campus. We strive to make Peiyang Garden Campus reflect and inherit historic culture, civilization and tradition, development level and standard in the future of Tianjin University and meet school-running target of world-class universities; reflect advanced level in the building field at home and abroad; reflect common aspiration of all teachers, students, and alumni of Tianjin University.

As a one-hundred-year old university, Tianjin University has cultivated more than 200,000 social elites for China in the past, who are important forces for development of Tianjin University. The new campus is constructed under concerns and supports of alumni in various regions and alumni at home and abroad support the development of the new campus in various ways. Every tree and bush of the new campus gathers wisdom and strengths of people in Peiyang University and Tianjin University. The future of Tianjin University is not only our future but also common aspiration of all alumni. I hope that alumni will be more united in the new campus.

"Fulfill Dreams of New Campus, Beginning a New 60-year Circle" means fulfilling the dream of Tianjin University in running university, making nation stronger, rigorous scholarship, and patriotic dedication. The construction and application of the new campus is an important milestone and a new starting point of Tianjin University, also a new starting point for us to make efforts. We shall insist in connotative development road of Tianjin University through grasping the opportunity of moving to the new campus, to improve the university' s comprehensive strength continuously and to build our university into a world famous university and a world-class university.

I hereby express heartfelt thanks to personages of all circles of new campus construction, all teachers and students, all alumni, and comrades making efforts on the front line.

Liu Jianping

August, 2015

序二

从北洋大学堂到天津大学，这所跨越3个世纪的中国近代高等教育史上建校最早的高等学府，将于2015年10月2日迎来120周年双甲子校庆。

20世纪50年代，天津大学由西沽旧址迁至南开区七里台卫津路校址，是当时和后来较长时期国内规模最大的多学科性工业大学之一。自20世纪90年代以来，随着招生规模的扩大、新学科的建设，办学空间不足已成为制约学校事业发展的主要瓶颈。与此同时，国内许多兄弟院校通过调整合并、建设新校区，扩大了办学空间，改善了办学环境和条件，科研、教学等各项事业快速发展。

20世纪90年代开始，天津大学有过数次筹建新校区的努力，都没有成功。在教育部和天津市的大力支持下，2009年学校启动了新校区建设筹划工作。2010年和2011年，教育部与天津市两次签署合作协议，重点共建天津大学、南开大学新校区。天津大学新校区位于津南区海河中游南岸，海河教育园区内，占地3750亩，由天津市无偿划拨。新校区坐落之地附近有个村庄叫北洋村，而老校区东门前潺潺流过的卫津河，蜿蜒城市数十里仍然流经新校区。冥冥之中，似有天意。我们把这里定名为“北洋园”校区，希望能够在这片新土地上承袭天大百廿年的历史文脉和人文精神，延续“兴学强国”“实事求是”的北洋魂。2013年5月18日，新校区第一座建筑——图书馆破土动工。至2015年9月，一期工程90万平方米（22个建筑组团）已经全部完工，通过验收，投入使用。一座美丽、现代的新校区屹立在北洋园，北洋大学—天津大学站在了新的历史起点上。

新校区规划建设之初，学校成立了规划工作营，邀请了一批建筑领域的杰出校友加入。正如这本规划建设实录中所展示的，新校区的大多数单体建筑都由我们自己的校友完成的。这本规划建设实录，记录了设计大师们为新校区规划建设不断优化方案、凝聚思想的点滴，体现了新校区以学生成长为中心的规划建设理念的形成过程。

2010年，学校成立了新校区建设领导小组和新校区建设指挥部，并于2012年合并组建了新校区规划建设管理办公室，一批精兵强将从学校基建处和有关部门抽调进入指挥部和办公室。他们饱含热情，日夜工作在建设第一线。

新校区的建设，洒下了广大建设者的辛勤汗水，也得到了海内外校友和社会各界人士的高度关注和热情支持。在此，我代表全校师生向辛勤奋战在新校区建设第一线的同志们致以崇高的敬意！向为新校区建设贡献智慧和力量的校友们和朋友们表示衷心的感谢！

李家俊

2015年8月

Preface 2

The earliest institution of higher education in modern China for stepping over three centuries, from Peiyang University to Tianjin University, will welcome its 120th anniversary on October 2nd, 2015.

Tianjin University removed from Xigu to Weijin Road, Qilitai, Nankai District in the 1950s. It was one of the largest multidisciplinary polytechnic universities in China at that time and later on. However, since 1990s, with expansion of enrollment scale and construction of new discipline, insufficient school-running space has become the main bottleneck restraining the university' s development. And at the same time, many brother universities in China have improved school-running environment and conditions through adjustment, merger, and construction of the new campus, whose scientific research and teaching have developed rapidly.

Tianjin University has tried to construct the new campus for several times since 1990s, but in vain. Strongly supported by the Ministry of Education and Tianjin Municipality, the university started construction planning of the new campus in 2009. The Ministry of Education and Tianjin Municipality signed cooperative agreement to build new campuses for Tianjin University and Nankai University in 2010 and 2011. The new campus of Tianjin University is located to the south bank of midstream of Haihe River, Jinnan District, within Haihe Educational Park, covering an area of 3750 mu, allocated by Tianjin Municipality for free. Finally, the new campus is located nearby Peiyang Village, and Weijin River flows through the new campus after meandering miles from the old campus. We name the new campus as "Peiyang Garden", hoping to inherit historical context and humanistic spirit of Tianjin University in this land and to continue the Peiyang Soul of "seeking truth from facts" and "constructing schools and making the state powerful". Library, the first building of the new campus, was started on May 18th, 2013. In September, 2015, the first phase project (900,000 square meters, 22 construction groups) had been completed, passed acceptance inspection, and put into use. A new beautiful and modern campus has stood erect in Peiyang Garden. Peiyang University — Tianjin University has stood on the new starting point of history.

In the beginning of the new campus' planning and construction, the university has set up new campus planning and work camp and invited a batch of outstanding alumni in building field. As shown in this book, most individual buildings are completed by our alumni. The book records deeds of designers for optimizing schemes for construction planning of the new campus and embodies the forming process of student-centered planning and construction.

The university set up new campus construction leading group and new campus construction headquarters in 2010, and new campus construction planning administration office in 2012. In addition, the university transferred a batch of talents from the Infrastructure Construction Department and relevant departments to the Headquarters and Office. They are enthusiastic at working on the front line day and night.

The construction of the new campus is the result of constructors' hard working, highly concerned and supported by alumni at home and abroad and people from all walks of life. I hereby express thanks to those fighting bravely on the front line of the new campus construction on behalf of all faculty members and students! I hereby express heartfelt thanks to alumni and friends devoting wisdom and strength to the new campus construction!

Li Jiajun

August, 2015

序三

继大规模高校合并之后，又掀起了一股强劲的兴建新校区的热潮。有幸，我曾先后应邀参加了近20所院校的新校区规划设计的方案评审工作。新校区的建设，对于每一所院校来说都是一件大事，因为它关系着学校未来的发展，受到校领导及广大师生的极大重视，并被寄予很高的希望。

地处天津的两所国家重点大学——南开大学和天津大学新校区建设起步较晚，似乎是这股热潮近乎冷却之后，方才启动，个中原因也有各种猜测，但无论如何，只要得以启动就会为学校未来发展创造极其有利的条件。况且，晚走一步还可借鉴兄弟院校的经验，把新校区建设得更加美好。

当今中国的大学，虽然规模有大有小，科系设置也有所不同，但从基本功能和组织结构方面看却大同小异，没有明显的差异和区别。因此，在校园规划设计中很容易出现趋同的现象。特别是到了后期，大学校区建设几乎陷于为数不多的几种模式。我校新校区的规划设计自然也很难跳出这种框框。

当时的校领导刘（建平）书记和龚（克）校长，在静观了一些已建成的新校区后，无意与之攀比，只是提出两点：其一是人性化，其二是体现北洋大学作为我国第一所新型大学所具有的文化意蕴和内涵。在新校区规划设计的方案竞标中，正是依据这两点而遴选出由天津华汇设计公司提供的规划设计方案。过了一段时间，华汇的总建筑师周恺同志认为该方案的中轴线过长，且与入口前的城市干道呈斜交的形式，于是建议在入口较近的地方使轴线有一个转折，这样，既避免单调，又便于入口大门的设计，于是，得到大家一致的认同，从而成为学校新校区总体布局的依据。

总体规划的实施在很大程度上还是要依靠良好的单体建筑设计。为此，大家提出以我校建筑学院毕业的杰出校友组成一个“工作营”，分别承担各主要单体建筑的方案及施工图设计。除此以外，还特邀了校友之外的一些优秀建筑师共同参与此项工作，经验证明，这种做法还是很有成效的。遗憾的是，由于项目的合并以及经费限制，致使一些较有特色的方案未能实施。

如今，新校区已经基本建成，尽管还有一些不尽如人意之处，但总体看来，在体现人性化，特别在弘扬北洋文化意蕴方面还是具有一定特色的。

彭一刚
2015年8月

Preface 3

After large-scale university mergers, the new campus construction is on the rise. Fortunately, I have been invited to participate in the review of new campus' planning design scheme of about 20 institutions successively. The construction of new campus is an event for each institution, because it concerns the future development, so that it is highly cared by teachers and students.

Nankai University and Tianjin University, two national key universities in Tianjin, started the construction of new campus late after cooling of such upsurge for many reasons. However, in any case, their start will create favorable terms for the future development of universities. In addition, they can refer to brother institutions to build the new campus more beautiful.

In the aspect of basic functions and organizational structure, current universities in China are largely identical but with only minor differences, without obvious differences, although they are different in scale and academic department. Therefore, it is easy to have convergence in campus planning and design. Particularly, university campus construction only has few models in the late period. It is difficult for our new campus' planning and design to jump out of such frame.

Secretary Liu Jianping and President Gong Ke just proposed two points after viewing some new campuses: one is humanization and the other is cultural implication and connotation possessed by Peiyang University, as the first new-type university. Just for such two points, the planning and design scheme offered by Tianjin Huahui Design Co., Ltd. (HHD) is selected. After a period of time, Chief Architect Zhou Kai of HHD thought that the middle axis of the scheme was too long and suggested to turn it in the place near to the entrance, which not only avoids being dull but also is convenient for the design of main entrance gate, and his proposal was approved by everybody. Therefore, it has become the basis for entire layout of the new campus.

To a large extent, implementation of overall planning depends on favorable individual building design. For this reason, outstanding alumni graduating from School of Architecture of our university composed a "work camp" to undertake design schemes and construction drawings of each individual building. In addition, some excellent architects besides alumni have been invited to participate in the project particularly, which is fruitful. Unfortunately, some characteristic schemes are not implemented because of project merger and expenditure limitation.

At present, the new campus has been completed basically. There are some unsatisfactory aspects, but it is characteristic in embodying humanization, particularly in developing and expanding cultural connotation of Peiyang University.

Peng Yigang

August, 2015

FULFILLING DREAMS OF NEW CAMPUS
BEGINNING A NEW 60-YEAR CIRCLE

Planning and Construction Memoir of the Peiyang Garden Campus of Tianjin University

圆梦新校区 启航新甲子

天津大学北洋园校区规划建设实录

Design the new campus for my Alma Mater

为母校设计新校区

今年是天津大学建校120周年。1895年中国第一所大学——北洋大学在天津成立，标志着我国近代高等教育的起源。为了迎接这个有特殊意义的日子，我们这些天大校友、北洋后人从5年前就开始参加了具有历史意义的新校区建设工作，从规划到建筑、景观、室内设计，从方案构思到工程设计到施工配合，无数次地前往老、新校区，数十次地参加各种会议，一晃，时间就在忙碌中过去了。

回想第一次应学校之邀讨论新校区建设计划，我们就提出邀请以校友为主体的集群设计模式，共同参与规划和建筑设计。这不仅可以集思广议，做出更好更丰富的设计成果，也是一个传承母校文化、延续母校文脉的具有历史意义的文化事件，当然也希望让校友们把对母校的情感、学生时代的记忆和对天大文化精神的领悟注入到新校区的设计之中。校领导十分支持这个提议，于是也就形成了全国新校园创作管理模式的一个创新点。

之后，学校便邀请彭一刚先生为新校区建设总顾问，天津华汇规划设计研究院黄文亮先生为总规划师，我出任校区建设总建筑师，周恺先生、张颀院长为副总建筑师，我们和主要校领导一起组成核心工作营，主要负责校区建设的设计组织和方案评审工作。另外邀请了中建院的李兴钢校友，天津大学的荆子洋老师，悉地国际的王海、王征校友，北京市院的姜维、王戈校友，日兴设计王兴田校友，墨臣事务所的赖军校友，深圳大学的覃力校友，远在加拿大的孟令强校友，天大设计院(AATU)设计团队，还有北京齐欣事务所主持人齐欣先生，都市实践事务所主持人之一王辉先生，北京大学王昀先生等组成了设计工作营。

设计之初工作营开过多次务虚会，主要讨论新校区规划设计的基本概念和原则。的确，经过十几年来全国大学新校区建设的热潮，有许多经验教训值得汲取和反思，已经形成某种套路的规划格局也似乎应该有所突破。为此工作营不仅进行了理念的讨论，而且还发动大家每人都画出校园规划的概念草图，充分展示出各自对新校园的畅想。经过较为深入的讨论和方案比较，最终选定了由天津华汇规划设计研究院黄文亮先生主笔深化规划，并由此提出了一系列核心理念并达成共识。

大家一致认同校领导提出的以学生为中心的理念，在规划中以一系列公共广场和庭院空间为主体，强调学生的活动是空间的主角，而不是一以标志性建筑为核心；我们强调紧凑型校园的理念，不仅是空间布局上可步行的便利性，更重要的是希望有利于促进学生以及老师之间的融合交流；我们强调校园的尺度人性化，不仅在于控制建筑的高度和体量，也关注室内外中小型轻松交流空间的营造，拒绝那种徒有其表、虚张声势、缺乏亲和力的“高、大、上”的建筑和环境；我们强调将功能混搭，让宿舍组团和教学组团相间并置，这不仅大大缩短了学生们上课的距离，也期许他们在学习和休闲之间可能迸发出来的创新活力；我们强调校园文化的传承，从纪念主题的诠释到水系景观的构建都取自老校区的特色，而从经典建筑语言的基调到砖石材料呈现出来的厚重也是老校区的气韵，更重要的是母校那种不赶时尚、求实创新的学术立场是我们格外珍惜的；我们还强调绿色生态，但这绝非仅仅依赖于节能技术的对标和堆砌，而更看重在设计中适宜策略的贯彻以及健康行为方式的引导；我们也很关注学校与未来城市发展的融合，一定为学术研究和创意产业发展以及相关社会服务留足空间，这也是校园可续发展的基本需求。总之，从这些基本理念和原则的设定，就似乎可以说已经与以往的所谓新校园规划范式形成了区别，走出了天大新校区自己的特色。

It is the 120th anniversary of Tianjin University this year. Peiyang University, the first university in China, was founded in Tianjin in 1895, which marks the origin of modern higher education in China. In order to welcome the day with special meanings, we, as alumni of Tianjin University and descendants of Peiyang University, participated in the construction of the new campus with historical meanings five years ago. From planning, individual architecture, and landscape, to interior design, from scheme conception to engineering design and to construction cooperation, we have left for the old and new campus for many times to participate in various meetings.

In the first discussion of the new campus' construction planning, we proposed to invite alumni to participate in planning and architectural design. By this way, we can not only make better and richer design results, but also inherit culture of Alma Mater, which has historical meanings. Of course, the university hopes that alumni can pour their emotion to Alma Mater, memories of school days, and comprehensions on spirit of Tianjin University into the design of the new campus. University leaders support the proposal completely, so that creation management mode of the new campus is formed.

Afterwards, the university invited Mr. Peng Yigang as the general counsel for the construction of the new campus, Mr. Huang Wenliang as the chief planner, me as the chief architect of the new campus, and Mr. Zhou Kai and Mr. Zhang Qi as the deputy chief architect. We and main university leaders composed the core work camp, mainly in charge of the design, organization, and scheme review for the campus construction. In addition, we also invited Li Xinggang, Jing Ziyang, Wang Hai, Wang Zheng, Jiang Wei, Wang Ge, Wang Xingtian, Lai Jun, Qin Li, Meng liangqing in Canada, design team of AATU, Qi Xin, Wang Hui, and Wang Yun ,etc.. to form design camp.

In the very beginning, the work camp has held several theory-discussing meetings to discuss basic concepts and principles of the new campus' planning and design. Really, after construction wave of new campus in national universities in the past dozens of years, we can learn from them and should break through certain established planning layout. For this reason, we have discussed on concept and everyone has drawn conceptual sketch of campus planning to show their imagination on the new campus. Through deep discussion and comparison, we finally chose the planning of Mr. Huang Wenliang. Based on this, we put forward a series of core ideologies and reached an agreement.

Everyone identifies with student-centered concept proposed by the university leaders, regarding a series of public plazas and courtyard spaces as the main body and emphasizing that students' activities are leading roles, rather than regard landmark buildings as the core; we emphasize the concept of compacted campus, to be convenient for spatial arrangement and to promote blending and communication of teachers and students; we emphasize measure humanization of campus, which not only lies in controlling buildings' height and mass, but also concerns on creating indoor and outdoor communication spaces, refusing gaudy, swashbuckling, incompatible buildings and environment; we emphasize mixing functions and alternate dormitories and teaching clusters, which can shorten students' distance to classrooms and stimulate innovation vigor during learning and leisure; we emphasize inheriting campus culture, from interpreting memory to building water system landscape. We particularly cherish the old campus' academic stand of not chasing fashion but being realistic and innovative; we also emphasize green ecology, which doesn' t only depend on piling up energy-saving technologies, but pay more attention to carrying out proper strategies in design and guiding healthy behaviors and ways; we also pay much attention to mixing the university and future city development together, leaving space for academic research, creative industry development, and relevant social service, which is also basic demands for campus' sustainable development. In short, it seems that setting such basic concepts and principles is different from previous so-called new campus planning ways.

黄文亮先生率领规划团队在综合比较大家的设计意图的同时，又提出了多达7个比较方案，最终确定的总体规划方案具有11个设计构想：1，东西向的校园主轴既巧妙地顺应了大规划格局，也使新校园大部分建筑争取做到南北朝向，而这也与老校区的东西主轴相呼应；2，营造以学生公共活动为中心的中轴空间，将校前区、公共基础教学区、图书馆以及大学生活动中心和北洋音乐厅分置轴线两侧，创造有青春活力的新校园；3，将现场排水沟渠改造成环形水系和校园景观，也有排碱，改善土壤的功效，有利于植物生长；4，功能分区以水系为界，水系内侧是公共教学岛，外侧则布置学院群落，既形成向内共享的学术交流平台，又向外延伸了对未来城市的服务功能；5，建设连通各个教学组团的交流通廊，这有赖于各个单体设计的响应与协调，最终形成多层次的、由街巷和庭院组成的步行网络系统；6，在教学组团之间错落穿插布置学生宿舍组团，每个组团沿河面布置食堂或具公共使用特性的空间，强调了环境的均好性；7，希望建立校际公交体系，并结合地铁和公交站点布置校际资源共享的商业或服务设施；8，均衡配置体育运动设施和场地，尤其结合环形滨水环境布置小规模的健康活动空间；9，在校园西侧和南北预留未来的成长空间，并与学院教学和科研功能相衔接，以适合学科的发展需求；10，综合性地采用成熟的节能环保技术，尤其是将雨水收集和污水处理净化与景观设计一体化考虑；11，传承老校区传统砖建筑特色，采用地方材料页岩空心砖砌筑外墙，希望打造有长久价值的百年校园建筑。

如此理性的规划得到了各方面的一致认可，总体格局很快确定下来，但是校前区的方案却碰到难题：由于主校门处于东南侧大学城的景观路上，与东西向的校园主轴偏转了19.5度，就如何过渡这个轴线的转换进行了长达近一年的方案推敲。开始的环形林荫道方案以大草坪作为校前区，环形路完成了轴线的转变，但从校门到主建筑群距离偏长；后来在轴线上加了校史馆，并以标志塔为轴转换方向，但似乎纪念性建筑作为校前区的主体也不太合适；最终的转机还是来自华汇对规划格局的调整，将轴线的转折点后移，让校前区建筑群转向东南与校门对位，并将原来分别设于两侧的北洋会堂和文、理学院组团集中呈一字形布置，把行政楼移到空间转换区的三角绿地的北边，这个难题才得到了破解。

其实在规划调整优化过程中，各个建筑师团队已经按分工投入了设计工作。校前区北侧是荆子洋老师设计的行政楼，其主要特色是入口门廊处高大的柱阵，精心推敲的构成关系显示出经典的力度，后来因为规划调整将其移到化工学院旁边，对着三角绿地，但方案格局和形态没变。校前区南侧原来请王辉先生设计北洋会堂，他非常认真，提出了多个比较方案，还经过了多次修改，但后来因为规划调整而取消。同样遇到这种情况的还有张颀院长和覃力校友，他们分别设计了理科和文科组团，也分别位于主轴线两侧，方案都采用了围合式布局，在设计手法上文学院更多了一些文化性的表达，理学院则更理性、现代些，这些手法在后来的设计中都有所借鉴。我承担了中心岛上公共教学区两个实验楼和计算机中心的设计，方案的想法是想充分利用沿河景观的优势多创造一些开敞空间，同时适当分解体量，形成比较亲切的尺度，而一方一圆两个入口空间也成为进入核心岛的“桥头堡”。悉地国际赵晓钧校友派出两位得力干将王海校友和王征校友，分别设计中轴两侧的公共教学楼和其外侧的宿舍组团，教学楼采用了与实验楼类似的手法，在中轴路两侧形成了有节奏的小体量建筑，尺度比较亲切。再向前就是周恺校友承担的图书馆及相邻教学组团设计，其位置处于公共教学区的核心位置，跨越东西向主轴线，是整体校园的中心和标志，原本也规划为校园最高点，45米高，但是经过研究和比较，最终周总选择了水平展开的方院格局，并精心设计了前后架空门廊，让主轴线穿过图书馆延伸到湖边广场，整座建筑表现出低调内敛典雅大气的文化氛围。穿过安静的图书馆庭院是广阔的滨水广场，广场南侧由来自加拿大温哥华的孟令强校友设计了北洋音乐厅和学生食堂，他采用流线型的体量表达了浪漫而舒展的情调，内部空间紧凑合理，外部空间与广场景观融合，手法十分洗练。广场北侧是大学生活动中心，由法籍华人建筑师齐欣先生主创，他以现代聚落的语汇表达了功能的丰富性，以金属材料和鲜艳的色彩强调了空间的活力。

环形水系外侧是学院和宿舍组团相间并置，其中机械和化工学院由天大设计院设计。机械学院入口前庭采用了非对称格局，强调空间的张力和宏大的尺度；化工学院比较中规中矩，以对称的格局强调其复杂功能组成的严谨性。王兴田校友负责设计水土建教学组团，其建筑的特点不仅在于外部立面比例典雅的柱廊，更有内在空间的层次感，给工程师的摇篮注入了文化性主题。北大王昀老师也曾参加了信息学院的概念设计，他通过调度几何主题使空间增加体验感的构思其实很有潜质，但可能因为使用功能上的问题选择了另外的方案，比较遗憾。北京市院姜维校友团队和北京墨臣赖军校友团队分别设计了两个宿舍组团，他们最初都设想利用底层架空和院落环境创造学生交流活动的场所，建筑形态上也比较活泼多样，力图改变一般宿舍区单调乏味的面貌，但最后可惜的是因为面积和成本的原因许多可贵的想法没有实现，但好在沿河都规划了食堂，这种公共空间的形态变化补充了宿舍面貌单一的不足。北京院王戈校友和帷邦设计公司张弛校友的团队设计了研究生宿舍，他们除了满足居住功能之外在构建南北向校园主路的街区空间上也做了不少研究。

Mr. Huang Wenliang has proposed as more as seven alternative schemes at the time of comprehensively comparing everyone' s design ideas. Finally, the overall planning scheme has 11 design ideas as follows. 1. East-west principal axis not only complies with the large-scale planning layout but also wins over south-north direction for most buildings in the new campus, which echoes east-west principal axis in the old campus; 2. Create the axis space with the center of students' public activities and place the university's front zone, public basic teaching area, library, student recreation center, and Peiyang music hall on both sides of the principal axis, to create a youthful new campus; 3. Transform site drainage escape canal into ring water system and campus landscape, to discharge alkali, to improve soil, and to make for plant growth; 4. The water system divides functional areas. Public teaching groups are located inside the water system, while colleges are placed outside the water system, to form shared academic communication platform and to extend service functions to future cities; 5. Establish communication vestibules to connect each teaching group, which depends on response and coordination of individual design, to form multilevel pedestrian network system composed by streets and courtyards; 6. Strew students' dormitories at random among teaching groups with canteens and other public spaces facing the river, to emphasize sharing of environment; 7. Build interschool bus system and arrange sharing commercial or service facilities with the combination of metro and bus stops; 8. Allocate physical exercise facilities and sites equally, particularly arrange small-scale health activity space with the combination of annular water environment; 9. Reserve future growth space in the west, north, and south side of the campus, link up teaching and scientific research, and fit for disciplines' development demands; 10. Use mature energy-saving and environmental-protection technology comprehensively, particularly consider rainwater collection and integration of sewage treatment purification and landscape design; 11. Inherit the old campus' traditional brick building features, lay the outer wall with the use of local material shale cavity brick, and hope to create centennial campus buildings with long-term values.

Such rational planning is generally consented by all, so that the overall layout is stabilized soon. However, the scheme of university' s front zone is in puzzle: the major school gate is located in the landscape road of university town in southeast side, diviate 19.5 dergree to the campus' principal axis of east-west direction. How should we transit the axis? In the very beginning, annular avenue scheme regards the great lawn as the university' s front zone, and completes transit of axis with ring road, but the distance from the school gate to the major building group is too long; lately, history museum is added in the axis, and symbol tower is regarded as the axial transformation direction, but it seems that it is improper to regard a commemorative architecture as the main body of the university' s front zone; finally, Huahui Group adjusted the planning layout, moving the axis' turning point backward, aligning at the building group in the university' s front zone at the school gate, arranging Peiyang Hall and School of Arts and Sciences on both sides, and moving the administrative building to the north of triangle green land on spatial switching area.

Actually, in the process of plan adjustment and optimization, architect groups have worked on design by division of labor. The administrative building designed by Teacher Jing Ziyang is located in the north side of the university' s front zone, whose key features are lofty pillars at the entrance. Elaborately thoughtful composition shows typical strength. Finally, it has been moved beside Chemical and Engineering School for planning adjustment, looking towards triangle green land, but scheme layout and form haven' t been changed. Originally, Peiyang Hall designed by Mr. Wang Hui was located in the south side of the front zone. He has proposed several alternative schemes and modified them for many times, but it has been cancelled for planning adjustment. Similarly, Dean Zhang Qi and Alumnus Qin Li have met such conditions. They have designed science and arts groups respectively, in both sides of the principal axis. In design method, Faculty of Arts has more cultural expressions, while Faculty of Science is more rational and modern, which are referred in following design. I have designed two laboratory buildings and one computer center in public teaching area of Central Island, to create some wide open spaces with the use of advantages of landscape along the river, to resolve mass properly, and to form relatively amiable scale, and a square and a round entrance spaces would become a "bridge tower" entering into the Central Island. Alumnus Zhao Xiaojun of CCDI has assigned two capable persons, alumni Wang Hai and Wang Zheng, to design public teaching buildings in both sides of the axis and dormitories outside it respectively. Library and adjacent teaching groups designed by Alumnus Zhou Kai are located forward, in the core of public teaching area, stepping over east-west principal axis, which is the center and mark of the whole campus. Originally, it has been designed as the peak of the campus, 45m in height. However, finally, through research and comparison, Zhou Kai has chosen the quadrangle layout and designed overhead porch, to show the whole building' s low-profile, restrained, and elegant cultural atmosphere. Passing through quiet library courtyard, people can see wide water front square. Alumnus Meng Lingqiang, coming from Vancouver of Canada, has designed a Peiyang Music Hall and student canteen in the south side of the plaza. He expresses romantic and stretched sentiment with the use of streamlined form, with compact and rational inner space and mixed outer space and square landscape. Mr. Qi Xin, a Chinese French Architect, has designed Student Recreation Center in the north of the plaza, expressing richness of functions with words of modern settlement and emphasizing space vitality with metallic materials and bright color.

Colleges and dormitories are located outside annular water system, where School of Mechanical Engineering and Chemical and Engineering School are designed by AATU. Asymmetrical pattern is adopted in the entrance of Mechanics Teaching Gruop, to emphasize space tension and grand dimension; Chemical Teaching Group is quite satisfactory, emphasizing the preciseness composed by complicated functions with symmetrical structure. Alumnus Wang Xingtian is responsible for designing Civil and Water Teaching Group, with elegant colonnades and layering intrinsic space, injected into cultural theme. Wang Yun of Beijing University has participated in conceptual design of Information School. He dispatched geometry theme to increase conception of experience sense. However, another scheme was used for functional issues. Jiang Wei of BIAD and Lai Jun of Beijing MOCHEN designed two dormitory groups respectively. They imagined to create students' communication and activity places with the use of pilotis and courtyard environment initially, in order to change cheerless appearance of common dormitory area. However, it is a pity that many valuable thoughts were not realized for area and cost. They planned canteens along the river, which supplements unitary dormitory appearance. Wang Ge of BIAD and Zhang Chi of Weibang Design Company designed graduate dormitories which not only meet the function of residence but also make up block space.

特别应该介绍的是中国院李兴钢校友设计的体育馆组团，他打破一般体育馆内向的空间模式，巧妙地把几个大空间并联串接，更衣室、淋浴室集中配套，并在其上设计了室内百米跑道，空间丰富，有体验性和互动性，特别是异型拱壳混凝土结构的应用表达了体育建筑的力量感，浑厚有力，应该是新校区建筑中最有个性和特色的。

应该说新校区设计中最难的还是校前区建筑群。如前所述，在规划阶段对这部分的空间格局、轴线转折、景观序列等问题就做过多方案的比较，当最终确定了规划方案之后，主要的问题就集中在主体建筑形象上了：到底是什么风格？如何体现标志性？当时市领导很关心校园建设，从风格上比较推崇欧洲古典风格，之前在北洋园的多所院校中都已采用了欧式形象，甚至为此还组织规划部门和天津大学、南开大学的相关领导考察了印度孟买大学。于是学校邀请了几家设计院做了十几个方案进行比较。实在地说，虽然作为天津大学的前身北洋大学的老校址的确有一座龙楼采用了欧式风格，似乎今天采用这种形象也是有一点儿文脉缘由的，但从校园文化发展的历史过程来看，无论是最早那座代表晚清洋务运动的龙楼，还是20世纪50年代徐中先生设计的中国传统风格的七里台校区建筑群，抑或是之后在校园中建设的许多现代风格的建筑都代表了不同时代的建筑文化，其中的一些优秀作品也是当时颇有影响的经典之作，成为我国近现代的建筑遗产。而如果我们新校区的主楼采用了欧洲古典风格，这毫无疑问是一种文化倒退，也不能反映母校求真务实、实事求是的核心价值观。好在这个方向没有再发展下去，设计又回到理性的轨道上来，经过几轮方案的比较，最终采用了以圆形广场为核心，以环形建筑为主体，以文学院和材料学院为两翼的组合院落式方案，既解决了校前区主轴线向公共教学区主轴线的转折衔接问题，也突出了以学生为中心的校园建设理念，还比较恰当地找到了造型标志性和空间实用性的平衡点。广场上的点睛之笔是彭一刚先生设计的北洋纪念亭，石亭并不在广场圆心位置，而是向北退让，由此形成的偏心式构图更增加了广场空间的动感，也呼应了轴线的变化，而高大的五边形柱廊庄重典雅，亭内安放着创始人盛宣怀的坐像，在天光辉映之下凝视着一代代北洋后人，而这个圆形广场也就命名为宣怀广场，成为百年大学的永久圣地。

景观设计是新校区设计中十分重要的组成部分，黄文亮先生的团队在规划之初就提出了一系列景观和环境空间的构想，什么地方植树，什么地方铺草，什么地方要有工整的仪式感，什么地方采用自然抑或生态的方式，以及如何立足于可循环净化的景观水系。随后天大环艺系的曹磊老师团队在此基础上进行了深化，增加了许多细节，使景观环境更融入校园生活。主轴线上的景观由于与之前规划在空间格局上有许多变化，而这部分强调景观与建筑的一体化，所以从主校门到图书馆一线的景观在彭一刚先生的指导下分别由我们中国院本土中心和天津华汇周恺的团队来深化设计。主校门方案也是难产的节点，之前有过许多方案，尤其北京校友会布正伟学长比较早的时候就提出了构思，但由于规划一直在调整中，校门内外的空间关系迟迟不定，所以最终没能落实，十分抱歉。最后结合已确定的护校河上的平桥方案和对已封顶的环形主楼的现场观察，大家都比较倾向大门更简单低调些。于是在讨论会上我即兴提出了卧碑构思，将桥面中央做成石板纪念甬道，延伸至校门处与校名坡墙连为一体，形成了刻在大地上的历史标尺，作为献给母校双甲子的纪念，这一想法得到了校领导和核心工作营各位专家的认可，而校门的设计最终由彭一刚先生主笔完成。校门后是花丛锦簇的升旗台，再向前是逐级下沉的跌水广场，水面西端的大台阶上有一方石刻的校徽，校友和来宾们将来可以在此簇拥着校徽背靠主楼合影留念。穿过环形主楼东向开口自然形成的大门就进入宣怀广场，以北洋亭为中心而形成的象征着年轮的地面环状铺装和树阵构成了内聚力很强的空间，成为校园的文化客厅。主楼的正西向有一道开缝，标志着轴线的方位，此处的大门洞就是通向主校区的入口。向前进入核心岛要过一座桥，桥设计呈双体双跨，中间嵌入一舢板状桥墩台地，希望它能成为同时具有交通和交流功能的行为空间。核心岛上的公共实验楼和教学楼之间是尺度宜人的林荫大道，树阵之间穿插了供师生课间交流的休息区，而林荫道的尽端便是周恺设计的图书馆。与造型简洁现代的图书馆建筑相比，周恺设计的庭院十分内向、安静和雅致，质朴的实砖铺地、高低不同的地台和高大的梧桐树阵营造了亲切的尺度和浓厚的书院氛围，与图书馆的气质十分吻合。主轴线最后的广场空间宏大，面对开放的水面和远处的山丘，可能寓意着走向绿色生态、面向科技未来的愿景吧。

但是，比起建筑的实施来说，景观设计的实现更需要时间的培育，那些按照图纸种下去的小树苗要长到表现图上的效果恐怕需要10年以上的时间。另外校园一期工程也还不能完全呈现规划的最终效果，许多项目还要经过多年的发展建设。换句话说，新校区要达到理想的状态也不是短期内可以完成的，校园的初步建成只是一个开始，更重要的是未来良好的使用和完善的管理维护，更值得期待的是随着时间的流逝，校园的文化在其中沉淀和滋养，一代代天大人、一届届天大学子也将在此扎根、成长，这无疑是一个漫长的、可持续的历史过程。

The gym designed by Li Xinggang breaks through introverted spatial pattern of common gyms, connecting several spaces in parallel skillfully. Changing rooms and shower rooms are designed intensively. With indoor hectometer runways, the space is rich and mutual. Particularly, application of arch-shell concrete structure expresses power sense of sports building, simply and honestly, which should be the most characteristic among buildings of the new campus.

I would say that the most difficult among the new campus' design should be the building group in the university' s front zone. As what has mentioned before, we have compared such part' s spatial pattern, axis turn, and landscape order for many times. After the planning scheme is confirmed, the primary issue focuses on image of the major building: what on earth is its style? How do we embody its landmark? Municipal leaders paid much attention to campus construction at that time, praising European classical architecture style and even organizing relevant leaders of planning department, Tianjin University, and Nankai University to investigate Mumbai University in India. And then Tianjin University has invited several designing institutes to do dozens of schemes for comparison. There is a Dragon Building in European style in the old campus site of Peiyang University, the predecessor of Tianjin University, so it seems that it can inherit cultural history if we adopt European style. However, seen from the development history of campus culture, the Dragon Building representing Westernization Movement in late Qing Dynasty, building group in Qilitai Campus of traditional Chinese style, designed by Mr. Xu Zhong in 1950s, and many buildings in modern style in the campus represent architectural cultures of different times. Some excellent works are classic at that time, becoming architectural heritages in modern China. However, if we adopt European classical style in the Main Building of the new campus, it is unquestionable that it is a kind of cultural regression, which can not reflect the core value of being realistic and pragmatic of Tianjin University. Fortunately, we didn' t develop in this direction and came back to rationality. Finally, we chose a combined courtyard scheme, with the core of round square, the main body of annular building, and two wings of Faculty of Arts and School of Materials, which solved the connection problem for front zone' s principal axis and public teaching area' s principal axis, highlighted student-centered campus construction concept, and found the balance point of modeling landmark and space practicability. The best point on the square is Peiyang Memorial Pavilion designed by Mr. Peng Yigang. The stone pavilion is not in the circle center of the square but to the north. Therefore, eccentric layout increases the dynamic of square space and echoes change of axis. Tall pentagon colonnades are elegant. The sitting statue of Sheng Xuanhuai is placed in the pavilion, gazing at people in Peiyang University from generation to generation, and the round square is named as Xuanhuai Square, the permanent holy land of Tianjin University.

Landscape design is an important part in the design of the new campus. The group of Mr. Huang Wenliang has proposed a series of conceptions in landscape and environmental space design in the beginning of planning; where to plant trees, where to sward, where to have neat and orderly ceremony sense, where to adopt natural or ecological ways and how to base on recycling and purified landscape water system. Soon afterwards, the group of Teacher Cao Lei from Tianjin University did detailed design, increasing many details, so that landscape environment blends in the campus life more. Landscapes in the principal axis have changed in spatial pattern, emphasizing integration of landscape and buildings. Therefore, guided by Mr. Peng Yigang, landscapes from the school gate to library have been designed deeply by China Architecture Institute & Research Group and HHD Group. The major school gate is a puzzle. There were many schemes before. Particularly, Bu Zhengwei of Beijing Alumni Association put forward the conception earlier. However, the conception was not implemented because the spatial relationship inside and outside the school gate was not confirmed slowly. Finally, with the combination of confirmed level bridge scheme on Nursing School River and on-site inspection on capping annular Main Building, everybody tends to simplify school gate. I proposed the concept of stele laying at the discussion conference, making tile-stone memory processional road in the center of bridge floor and extending to the slope wall of the university name, to form a historical scale-plate engraved on the earth, which has been approved by university leaders and core experts. The flag tower with flowers is behind the university gate, and gradually submerged water dropping square is forward. There is a school badge on the big step in west end of water surface, so that alumni and guests can take a group photo here. You can enter into Xuanhuai Square after passing through the gate. Ground cyclic pavement and trees with the center of Peiyang Pavilion compose the space with strong cohesive power, to become a cultural hall of the campus. There is a slotting in the west of the Main Building, which marks orientation of axis. The big entry here is the entrance to the main campus. In order to access the central island, it is necessary to pass a bridge, with two bodies and two spans, and a sampan-shaped pier is implanted, which can be used for transportation and communication. There are pleasant park avenues between public lab and teaching buildings in the Central Island, with resting area in the trees, and the library is located in the end of the tree avenue. Compared with concise and modern library buildings, the courtyard designed by Zhou Kai is introverted, quiet, and elegant. Simple bricks, high-low platforms, and lofty sycamore trees create amiable and dense atmosphere of academy of classical learning, coinciding with the temperament of library. The final square space of the principal axis is grand, which means moving forwards green, ecological, scientific future.

Compared with construction implementation, realization of landscape design needs more time. It may take more than ten years for small trees to grow. In addition, phase-I project of the campus can not embody final effects completely and many projects shall be developed and constructed. In other words, the new campus can not reach up to the ideal state in a short time. Initial construction of the campus is only a start, while favorable use and perfect management and maintenance are more important. As time goes by, Campus Culture will deposit here, and students of Tianjin University will take roots and grow here, which is an endless and sustainable historical process.

我们很荣幸能在母校的历史上写下重重的一笔，为天津大学绘制新的蓝图是莫大的荣誉和骄傲。为此，要感谢学校领导和广大师生以及校友们对我们的信任，感谢建校指挥部各位领导和同人对我们的大力支持，感谢我们各位参加新校区设计的优秀校友和同行以及他们身后的设计团队，也要感谢各个项目的施工总包和分包单位，没有大家的共同努力，新校区建设不可能在这么短的时间内完成，这是我们大家共同的作品！当然，尽管我们已经付出了很大的努力，但在快速的设计和建造过程中也难免会有不少缺陷和问题，实施的完成度也有待提高和完善，所以还不敢说我们已经向母校交出了令大家都满意的答卷，恳请大家给予批评指正。但是我们可以肯定地说，天津大学新校区设计对大学校园的教育模式和空间模式都有新的诠释，是有特色的。

以此献给母校一百二十周年华诞！

中国建筑设计研究院（CAG）崔愷 cuik61@aliyun.com

We are lucky and honorable to make a new blueprint for Tianjin University. Thanks to school leaders, teachers and students, and alumni for trusting us, to leaders and colleagues of University Building Headquarters for strongly supporting us, to alumni participating in new campus design and their design teams, to contractors of each project. The new campus construction can not be completed within such a short time without your joint efforts. We have made great efforts, but there have also been some defects and issues during rapid design and construction. Construction completion degree shall be improved. Therefore, we don' t dare to say we did well for it. Please criticize and correct us sincerely. Affirmatively, the design of Tianjin University' s new campus has made new interpretations on educational pattern and spatial pattern of university campus, which is characteristic.

Solemnly here dedicate to the 120th anniversary of our Alma Mater!

Cui Kai, CAG, cuik61@aliyun.com

目录

CONTENT

规划建设概况

Planning and Construction Overview

Planning and Construction Overview

规划建设概况

天津大学（北洋大学）始建于1895年，至今已走过119个春秋，将于2015年10月2日迎来双甲子华诞。在这120年里，天津大学（北洋大学）从梁家园博文书院到西沽，再到七里台，每一次校址的变迁，都成为学校事业发展壮大的难得机遇，如今天津大学再次落户津南，必将为学校的发展奠定更坚实的基础。

2009年，天津大学启动筹划建设新校区。天津市将天津大学新校区建设纳入未来十年城市总体发展规划方案，并选址于天津市津南区海河教育园区内，规划3750亩土地用于天津大学新校区建设。教育部和天津市委市政府高度重视我校新校区的建设，教育部为新校区建设投入10亿元建设资金，并在其他专项资金方面给予大力支持，天津市将土地无偿划拨给学校。2010年、2011年，教育部和天津市两次签署合作协议，重点共建天津大学、南开大学。天津大学学校领导班子高度重视，积极推进新校区规划建设工作，校常委会及校长办公会多次讨论新校区相关议题，形成了《天津大学关于建设新校区的决议》，并成立新校区建设的专门机构，强力推进新校区规划及建设工作。2011年2月，天津市政府第66次常务会议审议通过我校新校区总体规划方案。2011年12月20日，天津大学新校区奠基仪式在新校区新址举行，标志着天津大学新校区建设进入新的发展阶段。

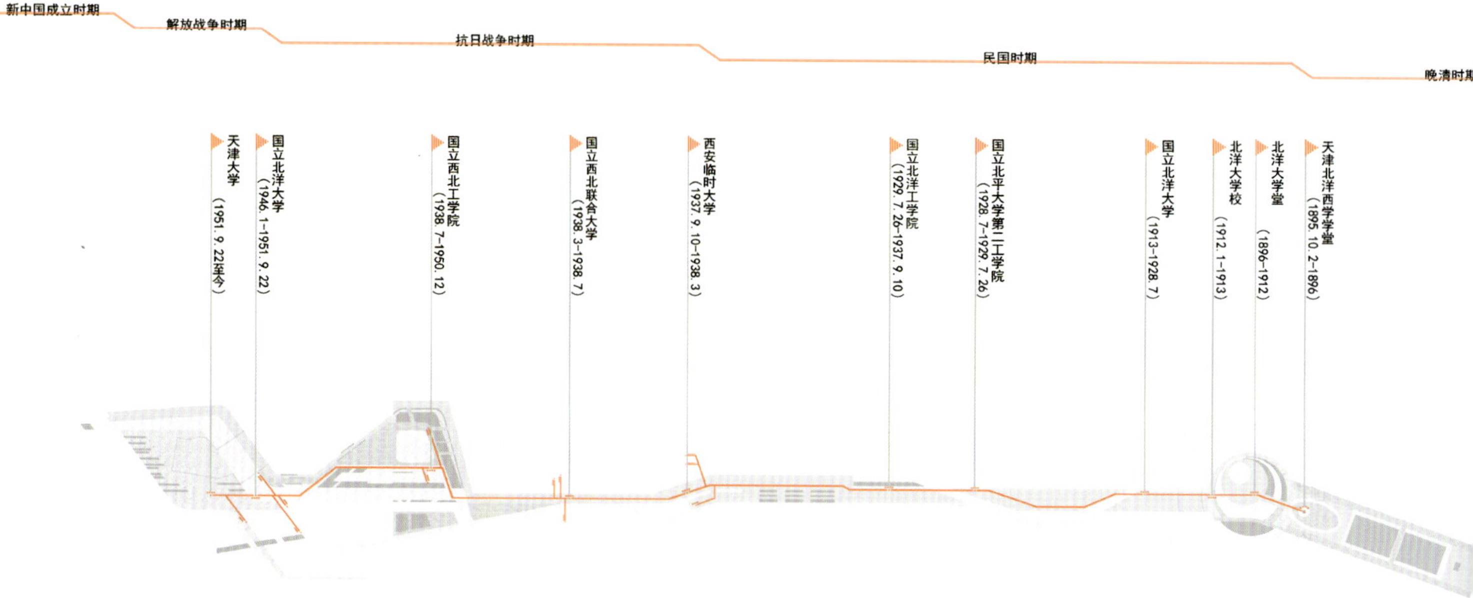

Founded in 1895, Tianjin University (Peiyang University) has undergone 119 years so far and it will welcome its 120th anniversary on October 2nd, 2015. Tianjin University (Peiyang University) has removed from Liangjia Garden Bowen Academy to Xigu and then to Qilitai. Each site change has brought rare opportunities to development and growth of the university. At present, Tianjin University settles down in Jinnan District again, which is certain to lay more solid foundation for the university development.

Tianjin University planned and prepared to build new campus in 2009. Tianjin government has brought new campus construction of Tianjin University into overall city development planning in the future 10 years, and chosen the site in Haihe Educational Park, Jinnan District, Tianjin, planning to use a land of 3,750 mu to construct new campus of Tianjin University. Ministry of Education, Tianjin Municipal Party Committee, and Tianjin Municipal Government pay high attention to the construction of our new campus. Ministry of Education has input a construction fund of RMB 1 billion for the construction of new campus and strongly supported the construction of new campus in other special funds. Ministry of Education and Tianjin government signed cooperative agreement in 2010 and 2011, building Tianjin University and Nankai University jointly as a key work. The university' s leading group has paid high attention to and positively promoted planning and construction of the new campus. University Party Standing Committee and President Office have discussed issues related to the new campus for many times, drawn up *Resolutions of Tianjin University on Constructing New Campus*, and set up a special agency to boost planning and construction of the new campus strongly. The 66th Executive Meeting of Tianjin Municipal Government passed overall planning scheme of new campus in February, 2011. Foundation-stone Laying Ceremony of new campus of Tianjin University was held in its new address on December 20th, 2011, which marks that new campus construction of Tianjin University has stepped into a new development stage.

Site selection and surrounding environment

选址及周边环境

北洋园校区选址于海河中游南岸，位于天津市中心城区和滨海新区之间，天津"双城相向拓展"的中心区域——津南区海河教育园区中部、生态绿廊西侧。用地范围东至海河教育园区纬二路、南至津港快速路、西至蓟汕联络线、北至海河教育园区纬六路。新校区距离老校区约23千米。天津大学新校区与南开大学新校区比邻而建，两校之间有1平方千米共享景观绿化带，两校分别位于景观绿化带的东西两翼。新校区北侧与多所高职院校临近，有利于资源共享，优势互补。

Peiyang Garden Campus is located to the south shore of midstream of Haihe River, between Central Urban Area of Tianjin and Binhai New Area, the central zone of Tianjin "twin-city opposite development" — the middle part of Haihe Educational Park of Jinnan District and the west side of Ecological Green Gallery. Its land range is to Wei'er Road of Haihe Educational Park in the east, to Jingang Expressway in the south, to Jishan Connecting Line in the west, and to Weiliu Road of Haihe Educational Park in the north. The distance from the new campus to the old campus is about 23km. New campus of Tianjin University and that of Nankai University are constructed neighborly, with a sharing landscape green belt of 1km^2 between these two campuses. The new campus is close to several vocational colleges to the north, which is in favor of resource sharing and the complement of each other' s advantages.

Planning objectives and functional localization

规划目标及功能定位

北洋园校区以"统一规划、分期建设、分步实施"的原则建设，总建筑面积130万平方米，其中一期建设90万平方米，包括主楼、图书馆、行政服务中心、学生中心、综合实验楼、公共教学楼、综合体育馆、各学生生活组团及各教学组团等22个建筑组团，2015年基本完成。一期建成后，12个学院以学科组群的形式实现整体搬迁，在校学生规模将达到21000人，教学科研主体功能将向津南新校区集中，卫津路校区将成为以高端培训、新兴学科培育、重大科技攻关和文化创意为主的特色基地。

Peiyang Garden Campus was constructed with the principle of "unified planning, stage construction, and implementation by step", and its total building area is 1,300,000 m^2. The building area of the first phase is 900,000 m^2, including such 22 construction groups as Main Building, Library, Administrative Service Center, Student Center, Comprehensive Experiment Buliding, Public Teaching Building, Complex Gymnasium, Living Groups of Students, and Teaching Groups, etc., which will be basically completed in 2015. After construction of the first phase, 12 colleges will move in the way of discipline group. The the number students there will reach up to 21,000. The main function of teaching and scientific research will move to Jinnan new campus, and the campus on Weijin Road will become a characteristic base giving priority to high-end training, training of new-rising subjects, significant scientific and technological research and culture creativity.

Planning thoughts and ideas

规划思路及理念

北洋园校区的规划建设与学校的办学理念、发展目标、历史文化风格及特色相适应，体现育人为本、学科融合、厚重纯朴、生态和谐、开放便捷等理念，着力打造人文校园、绿色校园、和谐校园、智慧校园。新校区总体规划体现“一个中心、三个融合”的理念，即以学生成长为中心，形成学科的集聚与融合、教学和科研的融合、学生和教师的融合。新校区承袭了天大现有校园的建筑格局，以东西中轴均匀划分校园空间，将公共教室、图书馆与活动中心等学生最常用的设施建在中心轴两侧，营造以“学生成长为中心”的公共活动空间，学生宿舍在中轴与学院组团之间错落布置，方便师生交流及学生学习生活。校园规划了“两河两湖一湿地”，沿校内运河设置环形生态景观园廊，延续了天大人对“湖”和“水”的记忆，同时生态湿地可以发挥净化污水、滞留雨水的功能，体现了“可持续发展”的理念。

Planning and construction of Peiyang Garden Campus adapt to the university' s educational philosophy, development goal, historical and cultural style and features. It embodies such ideas of cultivation-orientation, discipline integration, dignity and simplicity, ecological harmony, and openness and convenience, making efforts to create humanity campus, green campus, harmonious campus, and wisdom campus. The overall plan of the new campus embodies the idea of "one center and three integrations", namely the center of student growth, gathering and integration of disciplines, integration of teaching and scientific research, and integration of students and teachers. The new campus follows the architectural feature of campus in Nankai District. The new campus space is divided by the central axis from east to west with the frequently-used facilities such as public classroom, library, and activity center standing on both sides, to create "student growth-centered" public activity space. The students' dormitories are well-arranged between central axis and college groups to promote the communication, studying and daily life. "Two rivers, two lakes, and one wetland" planned in the campus can extend the memory of people in Tianjin University towards "lake" and "water". And at the same time, ecological wetland can purify waste water and keep rain water, reflecting the idea of "sustainable development".

Create green and wisdom campus

打造绿色智慧校园

新校区在建设中采用云计算、物联网、融合通信、协同办公等信息技术，将学校的教学、科研、办公、管理与校园资源和应用系统进一步有机整合，打造智慧化校园。此外，第一公共教学楼按绿色建筑三星级标准设计，学生生活组团按二星级标准设计，其他建筑至少达到一星绿色建筑标准。校园绿色交通规划可实现中心岛无机动车的目标，并规划了校园巴士和公共自行车系统，营造“人行优先，自行车方便，车行可及”的交通环境。学校还特别构建了水资源循环高效利用体系，运用十级分层净化技术，实现雨水污水的再生循环利用。新校区建成后将达到国家绿色校园的标准。

The new campus adopts such information technologies as cloud computing, internet of things, integrating communication, and cooperative office, by integrate the university' s teaching, scientific research, office, management, and campus resource and application system, to create a wisdom campus. In addition, the First Public Teaching Building is designed as per three-star standard of green building, students' living groups are designed as per two-star standard, and other buildings are designed as per one-star green building standard. The new campus' green transport planning can realize the target of no motor vehicles on Center Island. Campus bus and public bike system were planned to create a traffic environment of "giving priority to human walking, being convenient to bikes, and being feasible to cars"; the new campus particularly built water resource cyclic efficient utilization system, to realize regeneration cycle utilization of rain and waste water with the use of 10-level layering purification technology. It will reach up to the standard of national green campus after construction of the new campus.

Seven features of the new campus —people-oriented, distinctive, and sustainable-development campus

新校区七大特色——以人为本、特色鲜明的可持续发展校园

特色一：充分体现了现代教育理念，中心区的学生宿舍布置，突出了以人为本、方便学生生活、以学习为根本的理念。

特色二：院系组团合理布置，体现了学科交叉与融合，沿学校外围布置的学院更便于大学服务社会的要求，同时形成面对城市社区良好的建筑形象。

特色三：规整的中轴线体现了天大自身文化的特色，成为面对历史、面向未来的空间载体，不至于产生新校区在校园历史文化上的断裂和零起点。

特色四：合理密集的路网规划为校园提供了多种出行方式，通过管理可实现学校中心区无机动车的目标和绿色出行的可能性。通过校园路网规划，可以为师生提供多种出行方式，未来校园内预计将建有机动车停车位9 800余个，自行车停车位3万余个。

特色五：土地利用集约，水体面积适宜，建筑面积适中，空间规划适度，具备可调整性，一期建设基本可形成功能齐全的主校区格局。

特色六：规划方案为学科的增长和学校的进一步发展留有余地，很好地体现了学校发展的可持续性。

特色七：分期建设，有序增长。

1. Full expression of modern educational concept. Students' dormitory layout in central part highlights the people-oriented first, students' life-convenience, and study-first ideas.

2. Reasonable layout of department groups embodies disciplines interaction and integration. Colleges around the university are more convenient for the requirements of university serving society, while the image of nice building is formed in face of urban communities.

3. Structured central axis embodies cultural features of Tianjin University, which becomes a spatial carrier for facing history and future, not producing breakage and zero starting point of the new campus in campus historical culture.

4. Reasonable and intensive road network planning provides several kinds of trip modes for the new campus. The objectives of non-motor-vehicle and green walking in central area of the campus can be realized. Through campus road network planning, several trip modes can be offered to students. About 9,800 parking spaces for motor vehicles will be constructed, as well as more than 30,000 parking spaces for bikes.

5. With intensive land utilization, appropriate water area, moderate building area, proper spatial planning, and adjustability, first phase construction can form all-around main campus pattern basically.

6. The planning scheme has left some leeway for discipline growth and further development of the university, which reflects the university's sustainable development.

7. Phased construction and orderly growth.

从空中俯瞰，新校区整体地形轮廓与天津大学校徽内部“北洋 1895”的盾形不谋而合，卫津路老校区前的卫津河蜿蜒城市23千米，又来到了津南区北洋园新校区，成为新校区护校河的一部分，种种因素都预示着天津大学将在这片新的土地继续发展壮大。古老的天津大学也将在120年华诞焕发新的生机，开启新的纪元，创造新的辉煌。

Overlooked from the air, overall terrain profile of the new campus happens to have the same view with the shield of "Peiyang, 1895" inside the school badge of Tianjin University. Weijin River in front of Weijin Road along the old campus winds for 23 km, to Peiyang Garden New Campus in Jinnan District, to be a part of School Nursing River of the new campus, which predicts that Tianjin University will continue to develop and grow on this new land. The historic Tianjin University will renew in its 120th anniversary, starting new era and creating new glories.

规划建设历程

Planning and Construction History

Planning and Construction History

规划建设历程

2008年

11月28日，天津大学和南开大学向天津市政府上报《天津大学南开大学关于尽快启动新校区规划和建设的请示》，建议将两校新校区建设列为天津市拉动内需的重点项目和2009年工作计划。天津市高度重视，中共中央政治局委员、市委书记张高丽，市长黄兴国都亲笔批示，要求把两校新校区建设和城市的规划布局一并考虑，并请熊建平和天津市规划局尽快提出意见。

12月26日，我校和南开大学向中共中央政治局委员、市委书记张高丽和市长黄兴国上报《天津大学南开大学关于新校区筹建工作的报告》，再次建议将“启动南开大学、天津大学新校区筹建工作”写入市委市政府2009年工作要点，并争取两校新校区建设项目进入国家拉动内需社会事业重大项目之列。

On November 28th, 2008, Tianjin university and Nankai University reported *Requesting Instructions of Tianjin University and Nankai University on Starting New Campus Planning and Construction Soon* to Tianjin Municipal Government, suggesting listing new campus construction of these two universities as major projects for stimulating domestic demands and the working plan of Tianjin government in 2009. Tianjin government paid high attention to the report and Zhang Gaoli, Member of CPC Central Committee Political Bureau and Municipal Party Committee Secretary, and Mayor Huang Xingguo wrote instructions to consider constructions of these two new campuses and urban planning and layout jointly and asked Deputy Mayor Xiong Jianping and Tianjin Planning Bureau to bring forward opinions soon.

On December 26th, 2008, Tianjin university and Nankai University reported *Report of Tianjin University and Nankai University on Preparing to Build New Campuses* to Zhang Gaoli, Member of CPC Central Committee Political Bureau and Municipal Party Committee Secretary, and Mayor Huang Xingguo, proposing to bring “starting preparation work of new campuses of Nankai University and Tianjin University” into the working focus of Tianjin Municipal Party Committee and Municipal Government in 2009, and striving for putting two new campuses construction into the project of stimulating domestic demands.

2009年

3月25日，天津市副市长熊建平牵头，召集各有关部门召开第一次两校新校区选址协调会。

6月17日，天津市委常委会同意选址方案。之后，天津市规划局3次协调两校新校区选址工作。

6月20日，天津市副市长熊建平召开了两校新校区选址说明会，听取两校意见。天津市规划局对两校新校区的选址方案作了说明。

7月13日至7月22日，《天津市海河教育园区规划设计方案》向全市人民征求意见。

7月21日到25日，我校由副校长刘东志带队，党委办公室和校长办公室、发展战略研究中心、学工部、基建处、天大建筑设计总院（AATU）及部分学院主要领导组成调研小组，赴浙江大学、上海交通大学、复旦大学、同济大学、南京大学、东南大学6所高校，就新老校区规划建设进行考察调研，重点对新老校区定位、新校区规划、新校区建设及管理、建设过渡期管理、经费筹集等几个方面的课题进行了学习和交流，对6所高校新校区建设的相关数据进行了整理，形成了《天津大学新校区建设调研报告》。

11月4日经学校八届党委常委会第50次会议讨论决定，成立了天津大学新校区规划领导小组。

On March 25th, 2009, Xiong Jianping, Deputy Mayor of Tianjin, took the lead in calling up relevant departments to convene the first coordination meeting about the two new campuses site selection.

On June 17th, 2009, Standing Committee of Tianjin Municipal Party Committee agreed the site selection scheme. Afterwards, Tianjin Planning Bureau has coordinated site selection of these two new campuses three times.

On June 20th, 2009, Xiong Jianping, Deputy Mayor of Tianjin, convened site selection explanation session to listen to opinions of two universities. Tianjin Planning Bureau has stated site selection scheme of these two new campuses.

From July 13rd to 22nd, 2009, Planning and Design Scheme of Haihe Educational Park of Tianjin sought for opinions from citizens of the whole city.

From July 21st to 25th, 2009, an investigation and survey group, led by Vice-president Liu Dongzhi, composed by party committee office and headmaster's office, Development Strategy Research Center, Student Work Department, Infrastructure Construction Department, AATU and main leaders of some colleges, went to Zhejiang University, Shanghai Jiao Tong University, Fudan University, Tongji University, Nanjing University, and Southeast University for investigating planning and construction of the new and the old campus, mainly learning and communicating the positioning of the new and the old campus, planning of the new campus, construction and management of the new campus, management of construction transition period, and fund collection, sorting relevant data of the new campus construction, and forming *Investigation Report on New Campus Construction of Tianjin University*.

On November 4th, 2009, Planning and Leading Group of Tianjin University New Campus was established through discussion on the 50th meeting of the 8th Standing Committee of Party Committee of Tianjin University.

2010 年

3月，教育部和天津市政府签署重点共建天津大学新校区框架协议，天津市将我校新校区建设列入全市重点工程和市委2011年重点工作全力推进。

4月15日，天津大学八届党委常委会第64次会议讨论决定建设新校区。

8月5日，天津大学新校区建设指挥部成立暨规划工作营开营仪式在天南大联合大厦举行，这标志着天津大学新校区的规划与建设工作正式启动。此后，我校开展了由国内外多家著名设计机构参加的新校区总体规划方案征集工作。

In March, 2010, Ministry of Education and Tianjin Municipal Government signed the framework agreement on establishing new campus of Tianjin University jointly. Tianjin Municipal Government listed new campus construction of our university into major projects of Tianjin City and key tasks of Tianjin Municipal Party Committee in 2011.

On April 15th, 2010, the 8th Standing Committee of Party Committee of Tianjin University decided to build new campus on the 64th meeting.

On August 5th, 2010, the ceremony of the establishment of Tianjin University new campus construction headquarters and opening of the planning work camp was held, which marked the planning and construction work of Tianjin University new campus starting. Since then, our university carried out overall planning scheme collection work attended by several famous design institutions at home and abroad.

2011 年

2月，天津市政府第66次常务会议通过了我校新校区总体规划。

12月，天津大学新校区奠基仪式的举行，标志着我校新校区建设进入新的实质性阶段。

In February, 2011, Tianjin Municipal Government passed overall planning of our university' s new campus on the 66th executive meeting.

In December, 2011, foundation stone laying ceremony of the new campus of Tianjin University was held, which marks that new campus construction stepped into a new substantial stage.

2012 年

3月，学校成立新校区规划建设管理办公室，强力推进新校区建设及规划工作。

4月，学校成立筹资工作小组，推进新校区建设筹资工作及自筹资金建设项目的招标工作。

In March, 2012, the university established Planning, Construction and Management Office of New Campus to boost new campus' construction and planning work powerfully.

In April, 2012, the university established Financing Working Group to boost new campus construction financing work and bidding work of self-raised capital construction.

2013 年

5月18日，新校区首个建设项目图书馆组团开工建设。

7月1日，新校区综合实验楼组团开工建设。

8月8日，新校区机械教学组团开工建设。

11月6日上午，天津大学新校区融资建设项目（一合同）计算机软件教学组团、第二公共教学楼、北区生活组团、中区生活组团、硕士生公寓组团开工建设。

11月26日，综合教学实验楼组团主体结构率先封顶。

11月，新校区融资建设项目（二合同）行政管理中心、东区生活组团、综合体育馆、化工材料教学组团开工建设。

12月12日，天津大学新校区融资建设项目（三合同）南区生活组团、博士生生活组团、水土建教学组团开工。

12月31日，天津大学新校区融资建设项目（五合同）主楼桩基工程完成招标，进入施工阶段。

12月底，机械教学组团、图书馆组团主体结构封顶。

On May 18th, 2013, the construction of Library Group, the first construction project of the new campus, was started.

On July 1st, 2013, the construction of Comprehensive Experimental Building of the new campus was started.

On August 8th, 2013, the construction of Mechanery Teaching Group of the new campus was started.

In the morning of November 6th, 2013, the financing construction project (contract 1) of the new campus including Teaching Group of Computer and Software, the Second Public Teaching Building, North Living Group, Central Living Group, and Living Group for Master students was started.

On November 26th, 2013, major structure of Comprehensive Experimental Building was completed firstly.

In November, 2013, the financing construction project (contract 2) including Administrative Management Center, East Living Group, Complex Gymnasium, and Teaching Group of Chemical Engineering and Material of the new campus was started.

On December 12nd, 2013, the financing construction project (contract 3) including South Living Group, Living Group for Doctor, and Water and Civil Engineering Group of the new campus was started.

On December 31st, 2013, bidding of major building pile foundation project for financing construction project (contract 5) of the new campus was completed, and it stepped into construction stage.

In the end of December, 2013, major structure of Mechanery Teaching Group and Library Group was completed.

2014年

1月20日，天津大学新校区融资建设项目（四合同）第一公共教学楼、学生中心、第三学生食堂、第五学生食堂完成工程招标，进入建设阶段。

4月29日，天津大学新校区主楼建设开工仪式举行。

7月1日，新校区融资建设项目首个教学组团——计算机软件教学组团主体结构封顶。

截至7月25日，新校区国拨及融资建设项目主体结构封顶建筑达50万平方米。

8月20日，新校区西区生活组团完成工程招标，进入建设阶段。

10月2日，天津大学119年华诞校庆纪念活动在卫津路校区和北洋园新校区先后举行，同时开启了以“圆梦新校区 启航新甲子”为主题的120年校庆系列纪念活动。

On January 20th, 2014, bidding of the First Public Teaching Building, Student Center, the Third Student Canteen, and the Fifth Student Canteen for financing construction project (contract 4) of the new campus was completed, and they stepped into construction stage.

On April 29th, 2014, construction commencement ceremony for Main Building of the new campus was held.

On July 1st, 2014, the major structure of the Teaching Group of Computer and Software, the first teaching group of the new campus' financing construction project, was completed.

Up to July 25th, 2014, the buildings for national funding and financing construction with major structure capping had reached up to 500,000 square meters.

On August 20th, 2014, bidding of West Living Group of the new campus was completed, and it stepped into construction stage.

On October 2nd, 2014, the 119th anniversary commemorative activities of Tianjin University was held in Weijin Road Campus and Peiyang Garden New Campus successively. And at the same time, the 120th anniversary commemorative activities with the theme of “fulfilling dreams of new campus, beginning a new 60-year circle” were started.

2015 年

5月18日，即将迎来建校120周年的天津大学正式启动了向北洋园校区的搬迁工作，机械工程学院金工实习基地的6台机床作为首批搬迁设备，承载着天大人的梦想从卫津路校区出发，并顺利落户新校区。

On May 18th, 2015, Tianjin University, whose 120th anniversary is coming, started to move to Peiyang Garden Campus. Six machine tools of Metalworking Base of School of Mechanical Engineering are the first batch of removed facilities, starting from Weijin Road Campus with dreams of people in Tianjin University and setting down in the new campus smoothly.

总体规划

Overall Planning

Overall Planning

总体规划

设计者

概念设计：黄文亮、钟增炜、刘莹、邱渺、李博、国嘉、林曦平
修建性详细规划：洪再生、王哲、王蕊、邵德超

Designers

Concept designers: Huang Wenliang, Zhong Zengwei, Liu Ying, Qiu Miao, Li Bo, Guo Jia, Lin Xiping
Detailed planning designers: Hong Zaisheng, Wang Zhe, Wang Rui, Shao Dechao

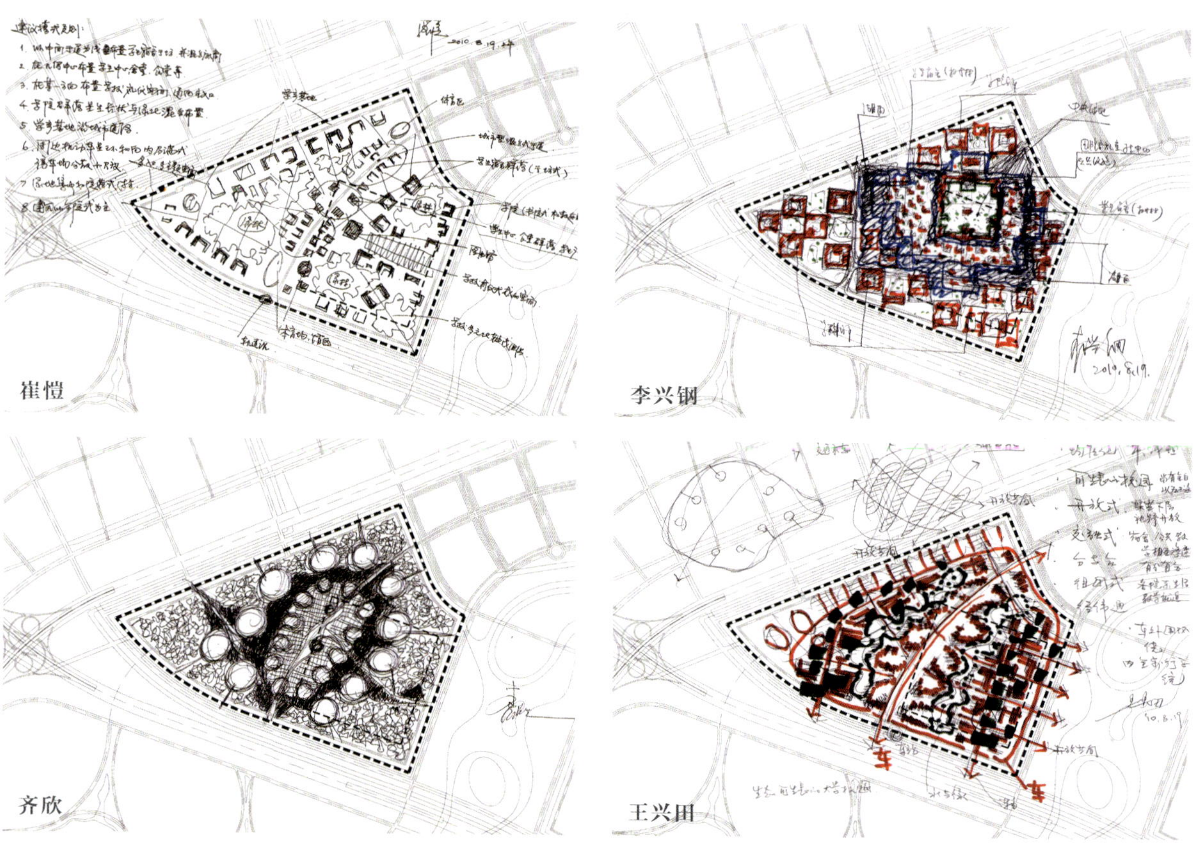

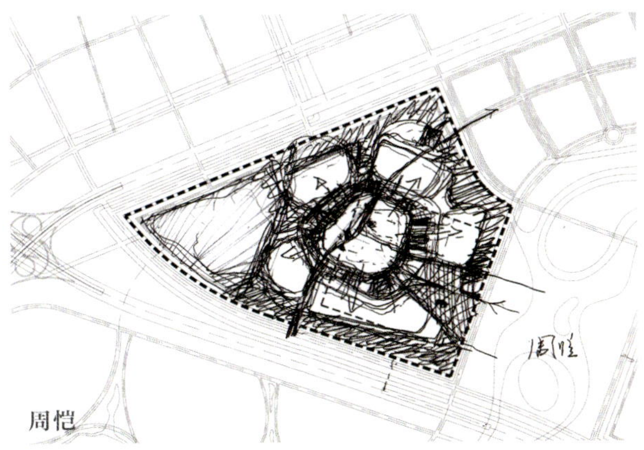

天津大学新校区规划用地250公顷，先期建设可容纳学生30000人，总建筑面积达130万平方米。在2010年新校区总体规划方案国际竞赛中，11位专家组成的评审委员会，包括吴良镛院士及彭一刚院士等大师级专业人士的评审下，华汇设计的“寻找大学之道”方案在5组国内外知名事务所中脱颖而出，获选为首选方案。

The planning land of new campus of Tianjin University is 250 hectares, The 1st phase can hold 30,000 students, and its overall site area reaches up to 1,300,000m^2 . In 2010 International Competition of New Campus Overall Planning Scheme, the design scheme *Seeking the Goal of University Education* of Huahui Group standed out and won the competition.

规划采用工作营方式推进，工作营核心成员通过一系列的工作会议，倾心聆听校园领导对学校发展的期许与愿景、管理单位对校园运营的需求、院系老师对教学研究发展的看法、学生对大学校园生活与学习的憧憬、具有深厚社会网络的校友对学校发展的倡议，以及天大杰出的规划设计校友与国内外顶尖专家们提供的宝贵的校园规划经验。规划团队整合各界建议，总结出“国际级现代化大学”的愿景定位，以及自主创新人才的发动机、可持续发展的领航基地、倡议和谐社会的智囊库等3个目标。同时规划团队依据工作营成果指认出可供参考的各种议题与策略，汇总专家提案后形成7个方案，再由校方及市领导经过慎重的商议，逐步建立最终方案共识。

With the use of work camp style, through a series of conferences, core members listen to expectation and vision of university leaders towards university development, demands of administrative institutions towards university operation, perspectives of department teachers towards teaching research and development, hopes of students towards university campus life and learning, propose of schoolfellow with profound social network towards university development, and precious campus planning experiences of outstanding schoolfellow in planning and design and top experts at home and abroad. The planning team has integrated and summarized the vision of "international modern university" and such three goals as engine of independent innovation, pilot base of sustainable development, and brainpower for proposing harmonious society. And at the same time, the planning team has appointed various referenced issues and strategies as per results of the work camp and formed seven schemes through summarizing experts proposals. The university authority and municipal government leaders have worked up final scheme through cautious negotiation.

The design adopts the main idea of one-step planning and construction by stages.
The three key points of planning and design are as follows.

设计采用一次规划、分期建设的主校区建设思路，重点有以下 3 方面。

1. 以学生为本的紧凑的校区空间结构

由本科生宿舍及服务学生的校园公共设施（包括图书馆、学生中心、音乐厅、公共教室等）构成紧凑的校园核心，各个学院环绕核心设置，形成校园外围的学术形象。研究生宿舍穿插安置在学院之间。紧凑的校园空间结构充分体现以学生为本的精神。

2. 串联学院强化交流的生态河

延续旧校园“有水则灵”的记忆，运用兼具排水滞洪功能的生态河道，以线形公园的形态环绕核心岛周边，串联各个学院，形成校园内师生生活交流的园地，落实教学与研究交融、学生与老师交融、学生与学生交融的规划目标。各个学院前，均设置开敞的“院埕”，在绿林间，散发各个学院的特质。

3. 体现大学之道的中轴空间序列

中轴线分为三段，三段共组 “大学之道，在明明德，在亲民，在止于至善”的精神。

1) 由校门开始至校前区的会议中心止，彰显天大历史的“明德段”；

2) 由教学主力设施及图书馆构成的“亲民段”；

3) 学生中心及音乐厅构成通往可持续公园门户的“至善段”。

1.Student-oriented compact campus space structure

The compact university core is formed by undergraduate dormitories and public facilities, including library, student center, music hall, and public classrooms, for serving students. Each college surrounds the core, to form an academic image around the campus. Graduate dormitories are arranged among colleges alternately. Compact campus space structure gives full expression to student-oriented spirit

2.Ecological river connecting colleges and intensifying communication

The new campus continues the memory of "spiritual water" of the old campus, applying the ecological river with drainage and flood detention function. Linear garden surrounds the Corner Island to connect all colleges in series, forming gardens for teachers and students on campus, to implement the planning target of blending teaching and research, students and teachers, and students and students. There sets open "courtyard" in front of each college, emitting characteristics of each colleges among trees .

3.Axis spatial sequence embodying the goal of university education

The center axis is divided into three sections. They form the spirit that "the goal of university education is illustrating illustrious virtue, being close to the people, and striving for perfection."

1) From the university gate to the conference center in the front zone, "Mingde Section" manifesting the history of Tianjin university;

2) "Qinmin Section" composed by teaching facilities and library;

3) "Zhishan Section" composed by the student center and music hall, leading to sustainable park.

校园分区图示
北区
中区
西区
南区
新元北路
明德北道
明德西道
明德南道
新元南路
北门
至善北道
规划界线
可用地界线
西北门（二期）
书园
校园建设用地界线
未来规划
新元北路
双台北路
平园23斋
平园24斋
平园21斋
平园22斋
第五十五教
计算机软件教
龙园
茅以升桥
日新园
亲民西道
明德西道
青年湖
学生中心
新元中路
双台中路
郑东图书
太雷广场
第四十四教
公共教
刘仙洲桥
治园19斋
治园20斋
治园17斋
治园18斋
第四十三教
水土建教学
西南门（二期）
新元南路
双台南路
御园
至善南道
第四十二
水土建教
第四十一
水土建教
南门
教学组团
功能性建筑
学生宿舍组团
食堂
主干道路（环路）
主干道路（纵路）
支干道路
桥梁及部分景观
广场
N

设计团队期待天大新校园在后续发展的过程中，能够把握国家面临能源及气候危机、文化传承难题、和谐社会维稳等严峻挑战的契机，“实事求是”地形成 “可持续观念与技术发展的先进平台”，为国家再一次肩负起新时代的历史任务。

Designers hope that the new campus of Tianjin University could master such severe challenges as energy and climate crises, difficulties in cultural inheritance, and stability of harmonious society, and form “an advanced platform for sustainable concept and technological development” practically and realistically, shouldering historical tasks of the new era for the country.

景观规划

Landscape Planning

School Gate Design

校门设计

设计者：彭一刚

Designer: Peng Yigang

设计说明

从海河之畔的梁家园博文书院到花堤蔼蔼的西沽，从艰苦卓绝的七星灯火到快速发展的卫津路校园，历史的车辙记录着天大校舍的每一次变迁，更见证着北洋大学—天津大学铿锵的发展脚步。校门设计秉承开放、平实、简洁的设计原则，同时注重内涵，又寓意深刻，学校120年历程，按特定的时间分为12个时段立碑铭记，石碑背面镌刻对应时间段的大事记，可称得上一座跨越世纪之门。

Design Specification

Each site change and development step of Peiyang University — Tianjin University has been witnessed in history, from Liangjia Garden Bowen Academy at the shore of the Haihe River to Xigu with flowers and from extremely hard and bitter Qixing Lights to fast-developing Weijin Road Campus. As for the design of school gate, they adhere to the principle of openness, nature, and conciseness and pay attention to connotation. The university has a history of 120 years, which has been divided into 12 periods and set up 12 monuments for memory, and great events of corresponding period are carved at the back of stone tablet, and it deserves to be called as a gate beyond the century.

天津大学

国立北洋大学

国立西北工学院

国立西北联合大学

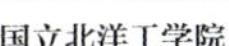

国立北洋工学院

国立北洋大学
第二工学院

国立北洋大学

北洋大学校

北洋大学堂

天津北洋西学学堂

Landscape Design in Front Zone

校前区景观设计

设计者：崔愷、冯君

Designers: Cui Kai, Feng Jun

设计说明

突出轴线精神

新校区的中轴景观规划体现了明德、求实、求知，迈向创新，止于至善的大学之“道”。

Design Specification

Highlighting axis spirit

Axis landscape planning of the new campus embodies pursuing virtue, being realistic, seeking knowledge, marching toward innovation, and striving for perfection.

收放有序的轴线空间序列

首先通过跨越护校河的连桥将两岸紧紧地联系成一个统一完整的校门入口空间，由柱廊围合出的入口广场将步行流线与车行流线分离。主轴线的步行林荫大道将人流引入校园，通过校名石和国旗将人流分散于水景两侧，视线随着层层向下的叠水交汇在位于中间的校徽上。在这里步行人流重新汇聚在一起，在主楼的衬托下校徽处成为历届毕业生合影留念的最佳位置。主楼围合出的中心纪念广场——宣怀广场是整个校园的精神所在，通过年轮般的层层景观元素突显着百年北洋之魂。经过主楼豁然开朗，一片自然景象映入眼帘。两岸的桃花使场所的气息回归到北洋大学的原址，轻巧的景观桥将学生带入求实求知中心岛。

Well-organized axis spatial series

Connecting both sides into an integrated school gate entrance space through bridge crossing school nursing river, entrance square (enclosed by colonnades) separates sidewalk and roadway. Walk boulevard of main axis brings stream of people into the campus and disperses the stream in both sides of waterscape through university name stone and national flag, putting line of sight on the middle of school badge along with downward stacking water. Here pedestrian flow gathers in one place again. Set off by the main building, school badge is the best place for graduates of all previous years to take a group photo to mark the occasion. The central memorial square enclosed the by the main the building —Xuanhuai Square is the spirit of the whole campus. The soul of centurial Peiyang is highlighted through layer-upon-layer landscape elements. It is suddenly enlightened after passing through the main building. Peach blossom brings the site breath into former address of Peiyang University. Students are brought to the central island of truth and knowledge seeking after walking through deft landscape bridges.

“刚”与“柔”的呼应

校园入口至主楼的轴线绿林环绕，造型恢宏，气氛静谧、安闲。通过校门、校名石、国旗、水景、校徽5个重要节点稳稳地落在轴线之上，书写着天大百年的治学精神。位于宣怀广场之中刻记天大精神、天大历史、天大校歌的北洋亭将中心景观引至高潮，同时成为了校园轴线的转折点，轴线轻松地转变为求实、求知的场所精神。在这里，开敞的滨水空间吸引着莘莘学子与先知学者谈学论道。

Echo of “hardness” and “softness”

The axis from campus entrance to the main building is surrounded by greenwoods, with grand modeling and quiet and comfortable atmosphere. The five important nodes on the axis such as school gate, school name stone, national flag, waterscape, and school badge show the scholarship spirit. Peiyang Pavilion located in Xuanhuai Square and carved with spirit, history, and school song leads the landscape to the climax. And at the same time, it is a turning point of campus axis, changing into a place for truth and knowledge seeking comfortably. Capacious waterfront space attracts numerous students and scholars to communicate.

景观个性的表达

场所的精神与不同的建筑功能相统一。天人合一的自然胸怀与传统的书院气质和理工的现代理性精神，天然巧妙地融为一体，打造成为真正以学生生活为中心、以学术活动为中心、以开放空间为中心的新时期校园精神。

Characteristic expression of landscapes

Site spirit unifies different building functions. Nature-human natural heart, traditional academy temperament, and scientific and engineering modern rational spirit integrate naturally and skillfully, to create a kind of new-period campus spirit with the center of student life, academic activities, and open space.

Peiyang Square

北洋广场

根据征集师生意愿和天大元素，沿用卫津路校区原命名。

The name continues to use the former name in Weijin Road Campus according to intentions of teachers and students and elements of Tianjin University.

天津大学

Xuanhuai Square

宣怀广场

以学校创办人、首任掌校人盛宣怀命名。盛宣怀，江苏武进人，曾任清政府邮传部尚书加太子少保，创办中国电报总局、华盛纺织厂、中国铁路总公司、中国通商银行、汉冶萍公司等近代重要实业，创建北洋西学学堂、南洋公学。1892年至1896年任天津海关道，1895至1896年兼任北洋西学学堂第一任督办。

It is named after Sheng Xuanhuai, the university' s founder and first leader. Sheng Xuanhuai, born in Wujin of Jiangsu Province, has ever served as Minister of Post-communication Ministry of Qing Government. He established important industries in modern times, such as Imperial Chinese Telegraph Administration, Huasheng Textile Mill, China Railways Corporation, Imperial Bank of China, and Hanyeping Company, as well as Peiyang Western Learning College and Nanyang Public School. He served as the officer of Tianjin Customs from 1892 to 1896 and the first supervisor of Peiyang Western Learning College from 1895 to 1896.

Sanwen Bridge

三问桥

参考天津大学历史文化元素命名，纪念学校杰出的掌校人张含英。

在原国家水利部副部长、原北洋大学校长张含英简朴的办公室内，悬挂着一张简易的条幅，上面是张含英自己题写的四个大字“实事求是”。而最耐人寻味的，则是他题在大字旁的“三问”：懂么？会么？敢么？这“三问”与其说是张含英写给自己的，不如说，是从北洋大学到天津大学师生一直都必须要回答的问题。张含英（1900—2002年），山东菏泽人，著名的水利专家，中国近代水利事业的开拓者之一，对黄河的治理与开发作出了不可磨灭的贡献。

It is named referring to historical and cultural elements of Tianjin University, to memory Zhang Hanying, an outstanding leader of Tianjin University.

In the office of Zhang Hanying, the former Deputy Director of National Ministry of Water Resources and the former president of Peiyang University, there is a simple scroll, where Zhang Hanying has inscribed “Seek Truth from Facts” . In the addition, there are “three questions” beside the scroll, namely “Do you understand it?Will you do like this?Dare you do like this?” Such three questions are not written to Zhang Hanying himself , but also must be answered by teachers and students of Peiyang University and Tianjin University rather only than. Zhang Hanying (1900-2002), born in Heze of Shandong Province, was a famous hydraulic expert and one of the pioneers in modern Chinese water conservancy cause. Zhang Hanying has made indelible contributions to controlling and developing the Yellow River.

donne une chance à la paix
中国近代的第一所大学
天津大学
实事求是
A VIBRANT CITY
COOPER RESERVOIR DEDICATED

自然的年轮

历史的年轮

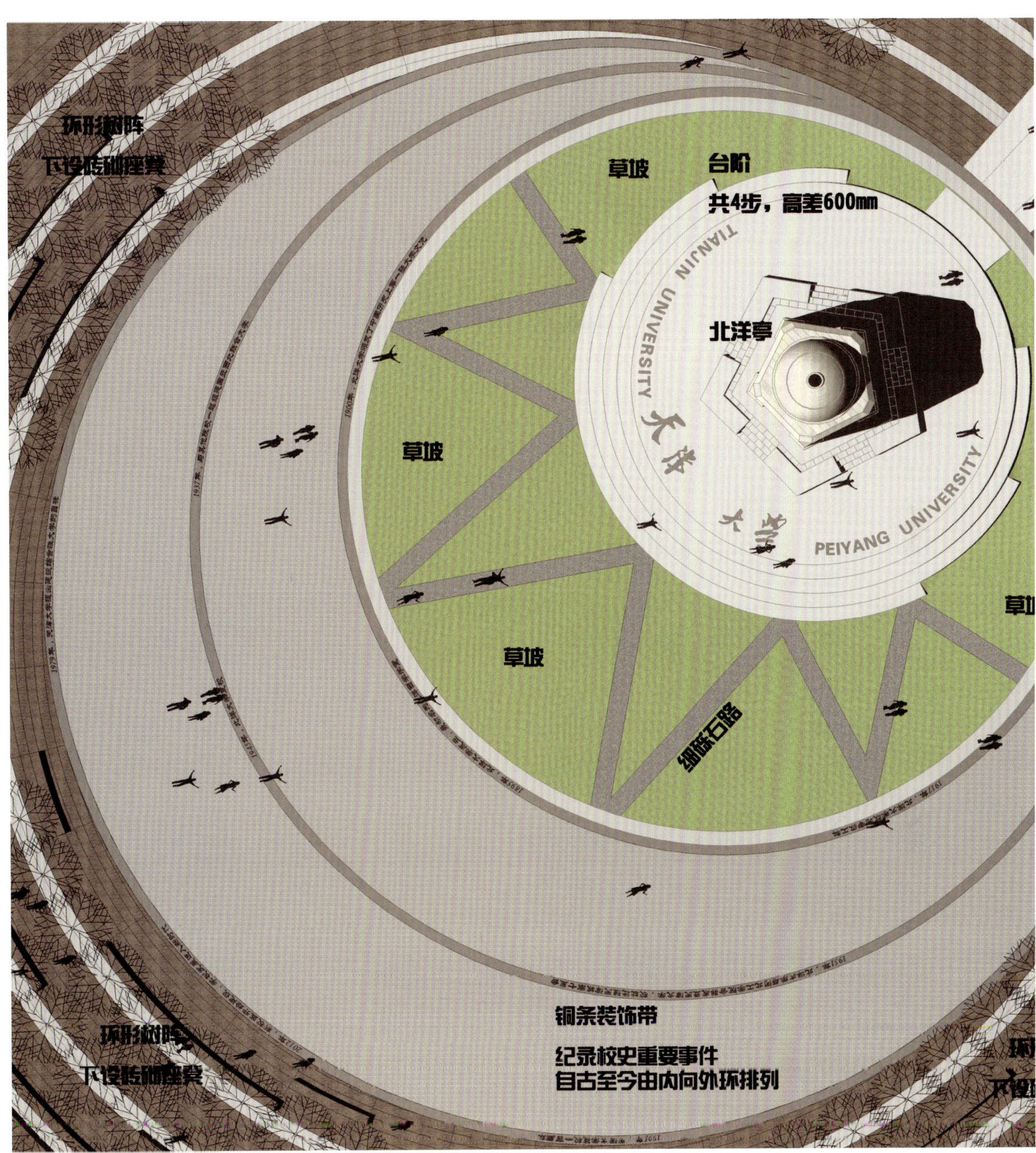

1895年，北洋大学成立，最初名为北洋西学学堂
1900年，北洋大学颁发了中国历史上第一张大学文凭
1917年，北洋大学改为专办工科
1937年，与其他院校一起组建国立西北联合大学
1945年，北洋大学复校
1951年，北洋大学与河北工学院合并成立天津大学，校址迁往天津城南七里台
1979年，天津大学提出建设综合性大学的目标
1995年，天津大学建校一百周年
2012年，新校区开始建设，学校发展进入新时代

Overall Landscape Design

总体景观设计

Concept of Design

设计概念

设计者：曹磊、王焱、宗飞、叶郁、代喆、席丽莎、沈悦、郝钰、高哲、张梦蕾、付建光、刘志波、王忠轩

Designers: Cao Lei, Wang Yan, Zong Fei, Ye Yu, Dai Zhe, Xi Lisha, Shen Yue, Hao Yu, Gao Zhe, Zhang Menglei, Fu Jianguang, Liu Zhibo, Wang Zhongxuan

设计说明

凝聚古树之茂密交错，汇集北运之水流滔滔，百年历史长卷用景观的方式展开，载历史之博大，育桃李之芬芳，续未来之辉煌。一轴串人文十景，一环连两堤六园，三石携君子六艺，两湖映南北六桥，三环六纵九支路，共喻历史之传承，展百年之筑梦。

Design Specification

Condensing dense and interlaced ancient trees and gathering surging flow, scroll over a century is unfolded in the way of landscape, carrying great history, raising fragrant peaches and plums, and extending brilliant future. An axis connects ten landscapes in series; one ring links two dykes and six gardens; three stonescapes take six art gardens; two lakes reflect six bridge; three rings, six vertical axles, and nine roads, explain historical inheritance and dreaming of one hundred years.

1. 以学生为中心。为学生打造适宜学习的幽静宜人的景观空间；打造优雅安全、适宜停留的休闲空间；保留可以聚会、庆祝的小型广场空间；预留充满活力、积极向上的体育活动空间。

2. 延续景观基因。血脉是北洋百年铸就的灵魂。天大新校区将蕴含延续传统基因血脉，以崭新的面貌面向世界和未来

3. 促进科学发展。琢玉树人，教育为本。新校区景观设计依据对学生需求之调研，以学生为本，整体布局营造多样、时尚兼具生态教育功能的空间。凝聚人气，促进交流。

4. 提升生态价值。绿色可持续是永恒的主题，在设计中依托规划条件，全面渗透“绿色、生态”理念。湿地、中心湖、溢流湖的布局实现了水质的提高与水资源的有效利用。

1. It is student centered: to create peaceful and pleasant landscape space for students; to forge elegant and safe leisure space, suiting for remaining; to retain small square space for party or celebration; to reserve energetic and positive physical activities space.
2. It continues landscape genes: blood is the soul of Peiyang created in the past one hundred years. The new campus of Tianjin University will develop traditional gene blood and face the world and future with brand-new outlook.
3. It promotes branch of learning development: education should be regarded as the foundation. In accordance with survey on students' demands, diversified, fashionable, and ecological-education space is created in the new campus of Tianjin University, condensing popularity and promoting communication.
4. It promotes ecological value: green and sustainability are the eternal theme. Fully penetrate the concept of "green and ecological" in the design depending on planning conditions. Overall arrangement of wetland, center lake, and overflow lake can improve water quality and utilize water resources

History and culture inheriting

历史文化传承

天大新校区将传承历史，同时为新土地注入新鲜血液。

The new campus of Tianjin University will inherit history and give fresh blood into the new land.

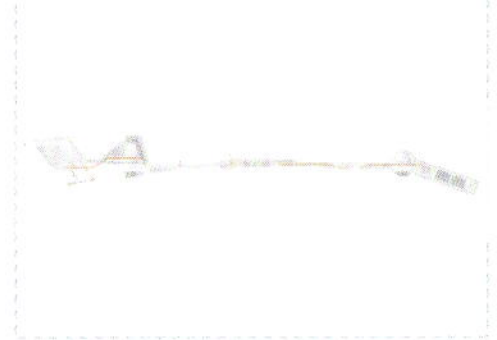

Carving jade and cultivating elitists

琢玉成器树挑李

教育之树人形同水流之琢玉，滔滔北运磨砺谦谦君子，蔼蔼花堤孕育天下桃李。

The landscape planning originated from jade. Educating people likes carving jade. The North Canal and fruitful flower dyke witness the growing up of the elitists of Tianjin University.

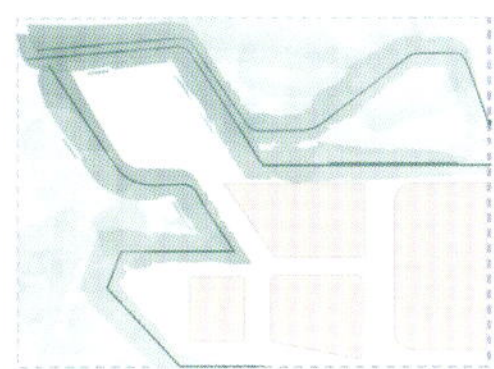

Taking a hundred years to educate people

百年树人

天大如同百年之古树，古树枝脉的生长有机整合各区块景观布局，脉络交织如同学科交错，蓬勃发展。

Tianjin University likes one-hundred-year trees, landscape layout of each block interlaces as disciplines interlace, booming.

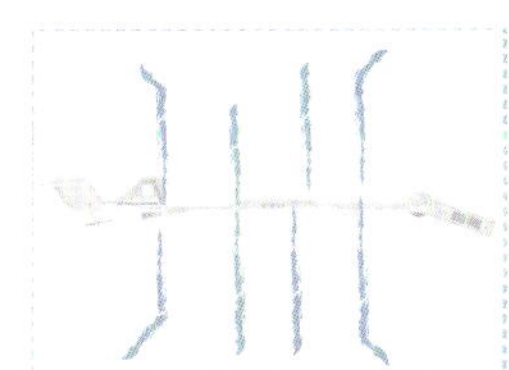

Gene interpretation of the old campus

老校区基因解读

天津大学既有校区景观格局主要为东西向轴线布局。中轴上分布有北洋广场、北洋亭、牛顿苹果树、敬业湖等景观节点。校园内还有四个人工湖，分别为敬业湖、青年湖、爱晚湖和友谊湖，湖水清澈，景色秀丽，清雅宜人。湖畔的垂柳堤、铭德道的海棠树也是校园中不可或缺的景色。

Existing campus landscape pattern of Tianjin University is mainly east-west axis layout. Peiyang Square, Peiyang Pavilion, Newton Apple Tree, and Jingye Lake distributed on the axis have become nameplates of Tianjin University. There are four artificial lakes on campus, namely Jingye Lake, Youth Lake, Aiwan Lake, and Friendship Lake, with clear lake water, and splendid, elegant, and pleasant landscape. In addition, willows on the banks and cherry-apple trees on the Minde Road are indispensable landscapes of the campus.

余晖映照下的校园

爱晚湖夏景

北洋道杨树林

敬业湖

畔柳堤
青年湖畔秋色
牛顿苹果树
北洋广场夜景
铭德道海棠
青年湖夏景
东西轴线鸟瞰
桃花堤
北洋广场鸟瞰
北洋大学堂
天津大学校门

Landscape Layout Analysis

景观布局分析

一轴。景观轴串起北洋广场、宣怀广场、三问桥、求是大道、天麟广场、书田广场、牛顿苹果树、太雷广场、青年湖、龙园湿地等10处人文景观。

One axis: the landscape axis connects ten human landscapes, including Peiyang Square, Xuanhuai Square, Sanwen Bridge, Qiushi Road, Tianlin Square, Shutian Square, Newton Apple Tree, Tailei Square, Youth Lake, and Dragon Garden Wetland.

两堤。校园南堤和北堤分别以桃花和海棠作为基调树种，是北洋老校区和卫津路老校区的隐喻，选用数十种海棠与桃类主题树种，植物丰富多样。

Two banks: capital trees in south bank and north bank of the new campus are peach blossom and cherry-apple trees, which indicate Peiyang old campus and the old campus on Weijin Road.

三环。三环包括内环河、中环路以及外环河。三环同时也是生态雨洪管理分区，倡导采用生态雨水收集方式，“源头”出发，分散处理，控制洪涝、净化利用，打造与环境相容的生态雨洪管理系统。

Three rings. Three rings include inner-ring river, middle-ring road, and outer-ring river. In addition, three rings are ecological storm-water management zones, conducting decentralized processing, and controlling flood, purifying and utilizing, and creating ecological storm-water management system which is compatible to the environment.

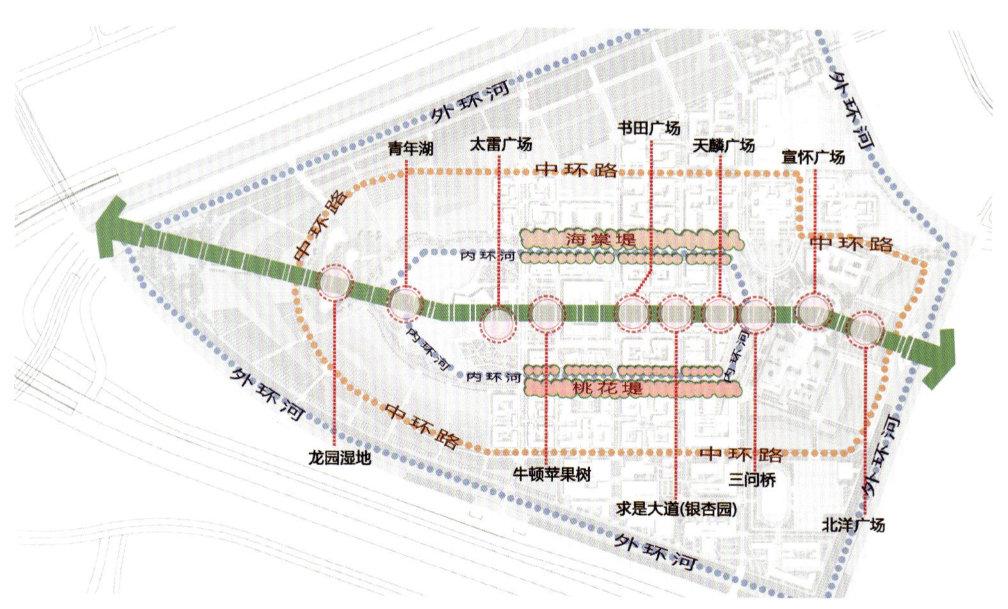

One axis connecting ten human landscapes

一轴串人文十景

在新校区景观设计工程中，保留原有设计精髓和空间氛围，并用新理念和新方法诠释和表现北洋大学和天津大学原有的校园景观特征和景点，使原有校区的景观基因得以延续和传承。

景观轴从北洋广场起航，穿越宣怀广场、三问桥、求是大道(银杏园)、天麟广场、书田广场、牛顿苹果树、太雷广场、青年湖和龙园湿地十景，展现历史，承接梦想。

The design should reserve original design essentials and space atmosphere in landscape design of the new campus and interpret and express original campus landscapes and scenic spots of Peiyang University and Tianjin University with the use of new concepts and methods, so that landscape gene of original campus can be continued and inherited. The landscape axis starts from historical Peiyang Square to Xuanhuai Square, Sanwen Bridge, Qiushi Road, Tianlin Square, Shutian Square, Newton Apple Tree, Qiushi Road(Ginkgo Garden), Tailei Square, Youth Lake, and Dragon Garden Wetland, to reveal history and to carry on dreams.

Qiushi Road(Ginkgo Garden)

求是大道(银杏园)

校训是一所大学的“灵魂”。以“求是”命名新校区中轴大道，旨在加强广大师生、校友及社会对“实事求是”校训内涵的认知和理解。

2010年4月，天津大学名誉博士韩国国会议长金炯午向天津大学捐赠了纪念树——银杏，象征着中韩友谊源远流长，银杏树作为特色树种植于天大新校园中。

School motto is the “soul” of a university. Naming the axis road of the new campus as “Qiushi Road” aims at strengthening cognition and understanding of teachers, students, schoolfellows, and the society on the connotation of “seeking truth from facts”.

Jin Jiongwu, Honorary Doctor of Tianjin University and President of ROK National Assembly, donated a memorial tree — ginkgo to Tianjin University in April, 2010, which indicates long-standing and well-established china-Korea friendship. As characteristic trees, ginkgo is planted on campus of Tianjin University to write china-Korea friendship continuously.

Qiushi Road
求是大道
Sanwen Briage
三问桥
Peiyang Square
北洋广场
Shutian Square
书田广场
Xuanhuai Square
宣怀广场
Tianlin Square
天麟广场
Tailei Square
太雷广场

Tianlin Square

天麟广场

天麟广场以北洋大学老校长、革命烈士赵天麟命名，以示纪念。赵天麟，字君达，天津人，1914年3月至1920年1月，出任国立北洋大学校长。 赵天麟任校长期间，总结北洋大学近20年的办学经验，概括出“实事求是”的校训，承袭至今。

It is named after Zhao Tianlin, once a president of Peiyang University and revolutionary martyr, for memory. Zhao Tianlin, also named as Junda, was born in Tianjin. He has taken the post of president of State-owned Peiyang University from March, 1914 to January, 1920. Zhao Tianlin has summarized schooling experiences of Peiyang University for about 20 years and the school motto of “seeking truth from facts”。

Shutian Square

书田广场

书田广场旨在纪念学校校史上杰出的掌校人李书田。该广场邻近图书馆，以老校长命名，有勉励师生 “以书为田，耕砚不辍”的寓意。李书田（1900—1988年），字耕砚，河北省昌黎人。1934年任国立北洋工学院院长。抗日战争期间，率北洋师生西迁，先后执掌西北联大、西北工学院等。抗日战争胜利后，1946年春率师生返津复校，担任国立北洋大学工学院院长至1948年。

The name aims to commemorate Li Shutian, an outstanding school leader of Tianjin University. The square is close to the library, encouraging teachers and students to study hard. Li Shutian (1900-1988), also named as Genshuo, was born in Changli of Hebei Province. He served as the president of State-owned Peiyang Engineering College from 1934. During the Anti-Japanese War, he guided teachers and students in Peiyang University to move westward. He has been in charge of Northwest University and Northwest Engineering College. After Anti-Japanese War, he, together with teachers and students, returned Tianjin to recover the university in 1946. He has served as the president of Engineering College of State-owned Peiyang University till 1948.

Tailei Square

太雷广场

太雷广场以学校杰出校友、革命先驱张太雷同志命名。张太雷是中国共产党早期的重要领导人之一，是中国共产主义青年团的创始人之一和青年运动的卓越领导人，是广州起义的主要领导人，1927年12月12日在战斗中牺牲，是中共历史上第一位牺牲在战斗第一线的中央委员和政治局成员。张太雷1915年12月以优异成绩考入北洋大学法律预科，于1920年毕业。

It is named after Zhang Tailei, an outstanding alumni and revolution pioneer, who is one of the important leaders in early stage of Chinese Communist Party, one of the founders of the Communist Youth League of China, an outstanding leader of Youth Movement, and a major leader of Guangzhou Uprising. He lost his life on December 12, 1927, the first Central Committee member and member of the Political Bureau in the history of the Communist Party of China who sacrificed. Zhang Tailei was admitted by Pre-laws Studies of Peiyang University in December, 1915, and graduated in 1920.

Newton Apple Tree

牛顿苹果树

英国科学巨匠牛顿因苹果从树上坠落而产生有关万有引力的灵感，是科学史上的一个传奇故事。这株苹果树也因此而声名大振，被视为科学探索精神的象征。2007年2月，由天津大学校长龚克率领的代表团到伍尔斯索普庄园，亲手剪下了“牛顿苹果树”的枝条带回国内。这株充满传奇色彩的苹果树被嫁接种植到天津大学，成为中国第一株直接引进的“牛顿苹果树”，供莘莘学子瞻仰。2015年3月18日，天津大学校长李家俊精心剪下“牛顿苹果树”的一根枝条，该枝条经冷藏、嫁接、培育后，与科学求索的精神一同“植”入天大新校区。

Newton, British scientist giant, had an inspiration of universal gravitation for falling of apples from an apple tree, which is a legend in the history of science. Therefore, the apple tree' s reputation has been greatly boosted, which is regarded as a symbol of scientific research spirit. The delegation led by Gong Ke, President of Tianjin University, went to Woolsthorpe Manor to cut off branches of "Newton Apple Tree" and took them to China in February, 2007. The legendary apple tree was grafted and planted in Tianjin University, which is the first directly introduced "Newton Apple Tree" in China. Li Jiajun, President of Tianjin University, cut off a branch of "Newton Apple Tree" on March 18, 2015, and "planted" it on the new campus of Tianjin University after being cooled, grafted, and cultivated together with the spirit of scientific research.

Youth Lake

青年湖

青年湖是老校区天大师生最喜欢的景点，是天大的名片。根据师生意愿和天大元素，北洋园校区的的湖泊沿用卫津路校区原命名，仍取名为青年湖。

Youth Lake in the old campus is the most favorite attraction and mark for students and teachers of Tianjin University. The new campus continues to use the former name of Weijin Road Campus according to intentions of teachers and students and elements of Tianjin University for the lake.

Dragon Park

龙园

1903年北洋大学堂教学主楼在西沽建成。因学校为光绪皇帝御笔硃批建立，新建的教学主楼的大门上方镶嵌带有皇权特征的团龙图案，故有“龙牌大学”之称谓。此外，湿地公园俯瞰有蟠龙之姿。综上，将湿地公园命名为“龙园”。

Main Teaching Building of Peiyang University was established in Xigu in 1903. The university was approved by Guangxu Emperor and the gate of newly built Main Teaching Building is inset with dragon pattern, so it is called as "Dragon University". In addition, the wetland park is like a dragon when overlooked. To sum up, we name wetland park as "Dragon Park".

One ring connecting two banks and six parks

一环连两堤六园

如水流之琢玉成器，同古木之树人育人，一环将两岸各个建筑组团联系起来。南堤，花桃蔼蔼，北洋园之再现，修园、齐园、治园等组团交相辉映；北堤，海棠争艳，天津大学的还原，平园、诚园、正园等组团相映成趣。

Educating people seems carving jade. One ring connects architecture groups on the two banks. The south bank with lots of peach blossoms is the reappearance of Peiyang Garden ,connecting Xiu Garden, Qi Garden, and Zhi Garden. The north bank with lots of cherry-apple trees is the restoration of Tianjin University, connecting Ping Garden, Cheng Garden, and Zheng Garden.

Peach Blossom Bank

桃花堤

1902年，北洋大学堂迁往西沽武器库旧址，学校师生在此种植了大量桃树。桃花堤、北运河一直是北洋学子心中的标志景观、历史见证者和文化符号。校歌中那句“花堤霭霭，北运滔滔”就是对桃花堤的盛赞。在新校区的景观设计中，结合自然条件和场地条件，又重新搭接了“桃花”与“天大人”的纽带，溯桃花之源。

Peiyang University was moved to the former site of Xigu Weapons Depot in 1902, where teachers and students planted a large number of peach trees. Peach Blossom Bank and Peiyun River are symbol landscapes, history witnesses, and culture symbols in the heart of students of Peiyang University, which have been praised in the school song. In landscape design of the new campus, "peach blossom" and "people of Tianjin University" are connected again with the combination of natural conditions and site conditions.

Cherry-apple Tree Bank

海棠堤

每年四月海棠花开的时节都是天大校园中最为浪漫而梦幻的季节——海棠季，铭德道旁列植的西府海棠已成为天大新的景观标识。海棠花是天大人共同的情感纽带，不仅因为它们那“偷来梨蕊三分白，借得梅花一缕魂”的醉人姿色，还因为其强大的环境适应能力。天大新校区的景观规划以海棠为基调树种，延续线形种植手法，并丰富了海棠的品种。

The campus of Tianjin University is romantic and dreamlike in the season when cherry apple trees beside Mingde Road blossom. The cherry-apple trees have become new landscape card of Tianjin University and common affection tie of people of Tianjin University, for not only intoxicating charm but also powerful adaptive capacity to environment. Cherry-apple trees are the basic trees on the new campus, by continuing linear planting and enriching variety.

Three stone-landscapes take six arts gardens

三石携君子六艺

Three stone-landscapes

三石景

设计分析了天津大学新校区整体及其周边环境情况，结合中国传统景观文化理论（风水学、环境学），浓缩出3个石景布局：其一是位于青年湖湿地景观环境中的一座叠石山景，将其作为新校区景观环境中心轴线的底景；其二是位于行政楼西北角位置上的土生石景观，造型如茂盛生长的尖笋状，冲天直上；其三是位于水土建教学组团中的土生石景观，外形仿佛灵动秀丽的山峰。三者共同构成了三足鼎立之势，祝福天津大学未来发展一帆风顺。

Overall and surrounding environment of the new campus of Tianjin University are analyzed, with the combination of cultural theories (fengshui theory and environmental sciences) of Chinese traditional landscapes. There are three stone-landscape layouts: firstly, a folding rocky mountain landscape located in wetland landscape environment of Youth Lake, regarded as the bottom landscape of central axis in landscape environment of the new campus; secondly, a native stone -landscape in northwest corner of administrative building, shaped as bamboo shoots; thirdly, a native stone-landscape in Teaching Group of Water and Civil Engineering, like clever and beautiful mountain peaks. They form a situation of tripartite confrontation jointly to bless smooth development of Tianjin University in the future.

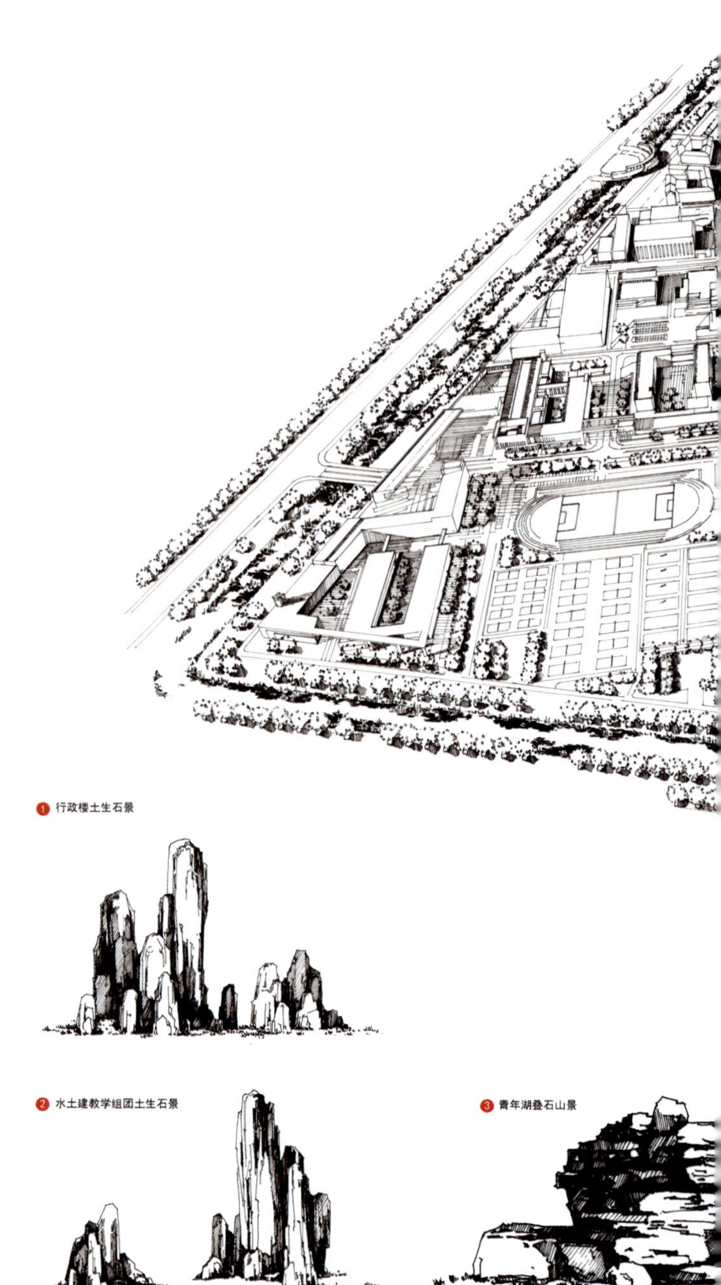

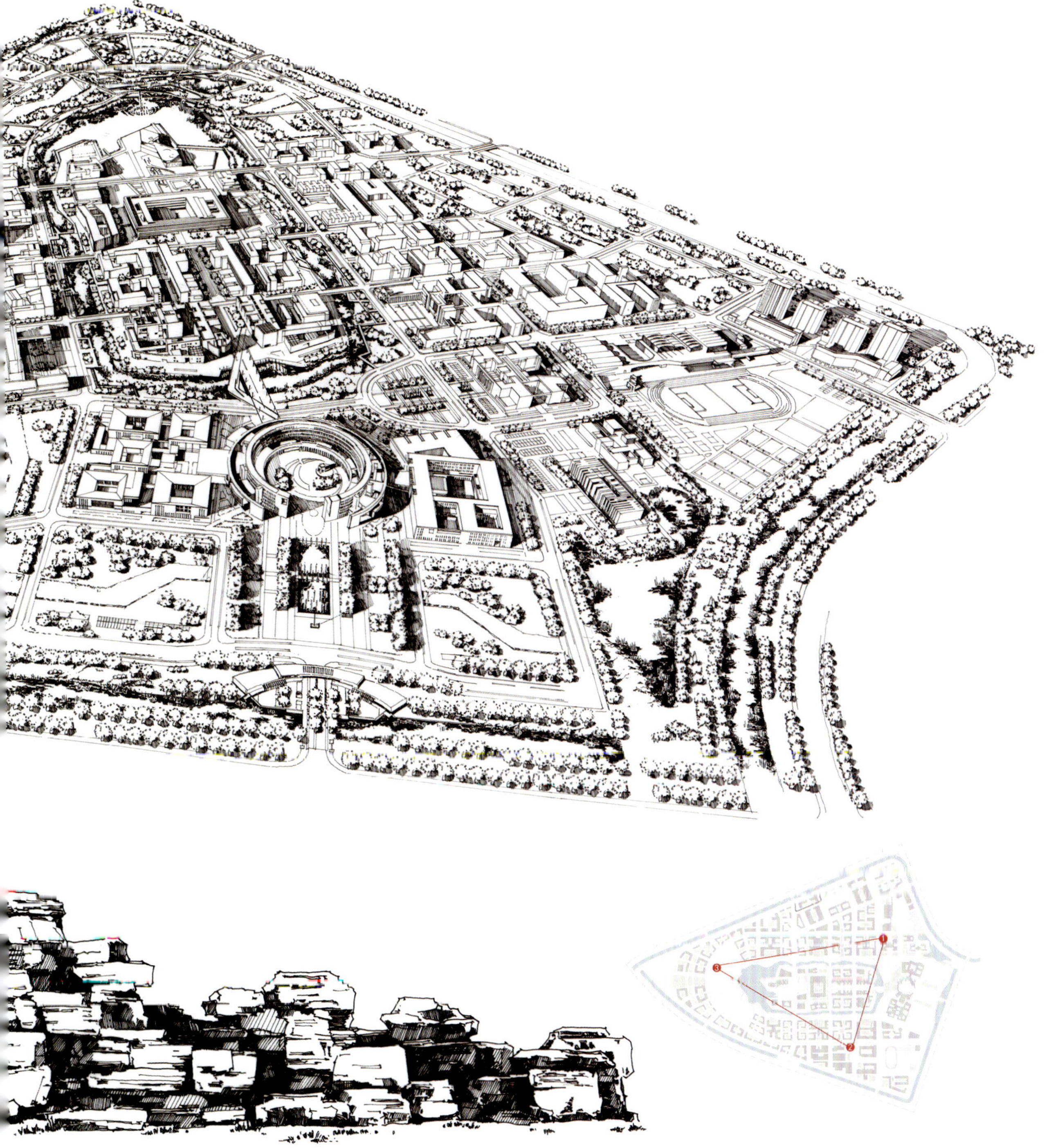

Six art gardens

六艺园

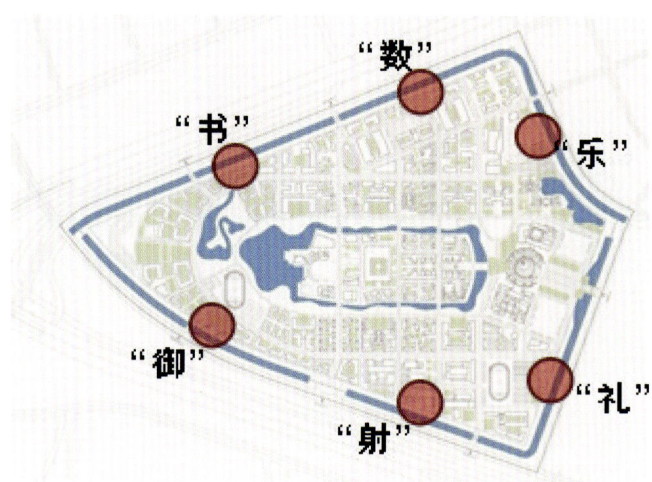

六艺是中国古代君子的六门必修课，内容包括五礼、六乐、五射、五御、六书、九数。赵天麟以“实事求是”作为天津大学的校训，不仅倡导了中国本土化的科学精神，还反映了他对中国传统教育的重视和继承。天津大学注重对学生综合素质的培养，这种综合素质的培养可被视为现代君子品性的培养，故取儒家经典《周礼》中的“君子六艺”为设计主题，结合校园外环线步道进行设计。六艺园为学生提供了更多的休闲活动空间。

Six arts are six required courses of gentlemen in ancient China, including five ceremonies, six musical instruments, five shoots, five driving tips, six categories of Chinese characters, and nine numbers. Zhao Tianlin regarded “Seeking the truth from facts” as the school motto of Tianjin University, which not only advocates Chinese local scientific spirit but also reflects his value and inheritance of Chinese traditional education. Tianjin University pays attention to cultivating students' comprehensive quality, and cultivation of such comprehensive quality can be regarded as cultivation of gentlemen's moral character. Therefore, the design theme is “six arts of gentleman” in The Book of Rites, Confucian classics, with the combination of outer-ring roads of the campus. Six Arts Garden provides more leisure activity space for students.

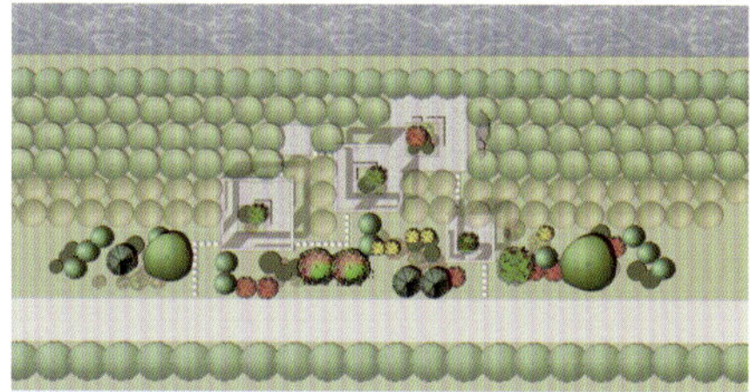

礼园
Li Garden

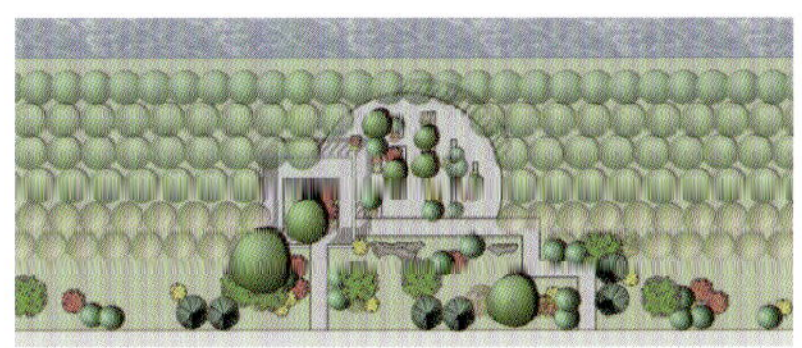

乐园
Yue Garden

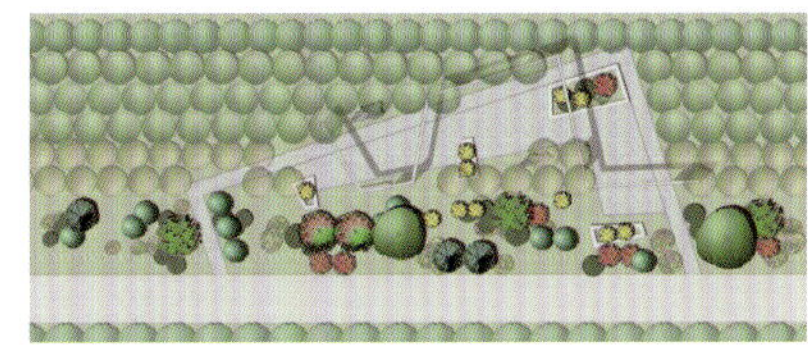

射园
She Garden

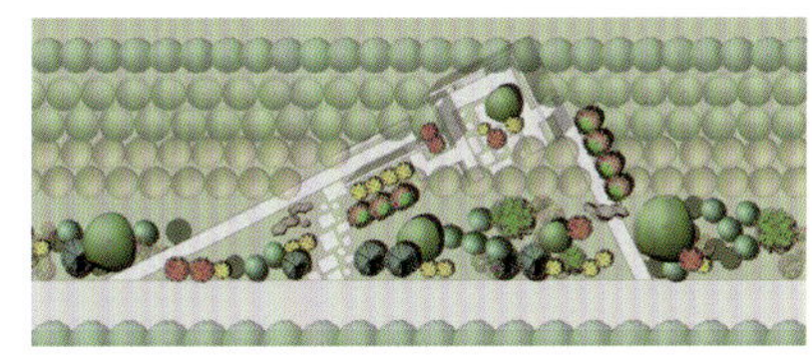

御园
Yu Garden

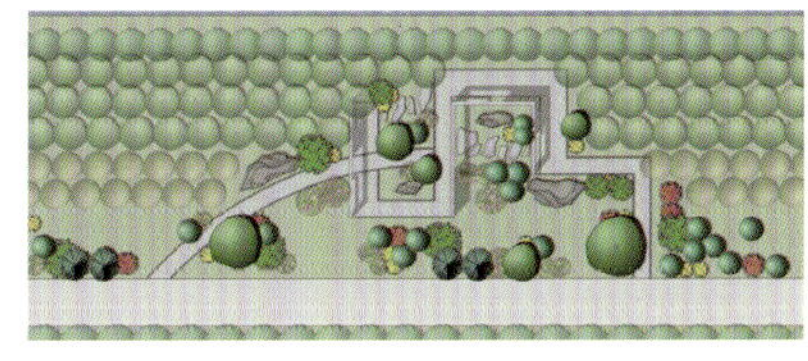

书园
shu Garden

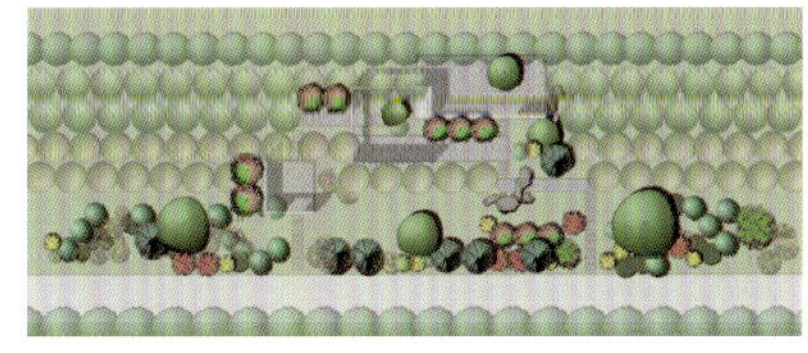

数园
shu Garden

Two lakes reflect six bridges on south and north banks

两湖映南北六桥

Two lakes

两湖

青年湖和敬业湖仍延续卫津路校区中二湖的基因，将为天大学子呈现一派“湖畔水景风光”，同时在打造生态校园中起到突出的作用。

Youth Lake and Jingye Lake still inherit genes of lakes in Weijin Road Campus, which will present beautiful lakeside landscapes and play a prominent role in creating ecological campus.

Six bridges in south and north of central area

中心区南北六桥

南北六桥以学校校史上建树卓著的六位杰出的掌校人命名，以纪念他们治学治校之成就、甘为人梯之精神。这六位掌校人按任职时间排序为：丁家立、王邵廉、刘仙洲、茅以升、张国藩、李曙森。

The six bridges are named after six outstanding university leaders who have made great contribution to the university, to memory their achievements in scholarly research and school supervision. Their time ordering for holding the post is as follows: Ding Jiali, Wang Shaolian, Liu Xianzhou, Mao Yisheng, Zhang Guofan, and Li Shusen.

Ding Jiali Bridge

丁家立桥

丁家立（1857—1930年），美籍著名教育家，协助盛宣怀创建北洋西学学堂。1895年至1906年任北洋大学堂（北洋西学学堂）第一任总教习，1896年至1908年任北洋大学堂留美学生监督。

Ding Jiali (1857-1930), a famous American educator, has assisted Sheng Xuanhuai in establishing Peiyang Western Learning School. He has ever served as the first General Teacher in Peiyang University (Peiyang Western Learning School) from 1895 to 1906, and the supervisor for returned students in USA in Peiyang University from 1896 to 1908.

Wang Shaolian Bridge

王邵廉桥

王邵廉（1866—1936年），字少泉，天津人，北洋大学第一任华人总教习，任职期间对校务严格管理，治学严谨，教授有方，“为学术努力，为教育尽瘁”，“处理校务措置尽当，富于责任心”。学校教师同人评曰：王‘有毅行，富果决，事之认为可者，绝不犹豫’。

Wang Shaolian (1866-1936), also named Shaoquan, was born in Tianjin, the first Chinese General Teacher in Peiyang University, strictly managing administrative affairs of the university during the term of office, making great efforts to academics and education, disposing administrative affairs of the university properly, and being rich in responsibilities. His colleagues evaluated: “Wang Shaolian was firm and resolute and didn’ t hesitate to approve things” .

Liu Xianzhou Bridge

刘仙洲桥

刘仙洲(1890—1975年)，河北完县人，1924年至1928年任北洋大学校长；机械工程学家、教育家、中国科学院学部委员；中国机械史研究的开拓者，对发展适合我国国情的农业机械作出了贡献。在教育上，倡导“工读协作制”的教育思想，自编我国工科大学第一套教科书，首先进行了我国机械工程名词的统一工作。

Liu Xianzhou (1890-1975), born in Wan County of Hebei Province, has served as the president of Peiyang University from 1924 to 1928. As a mechanical engineering scholar, educator, academic committee man of Chinese Academy of Sciences, and pioneer of Chinese machinery history research, he has made great contribution to developing agricultural machinery suitable to Chinese conditions. About education, he advocated the educational thought of “cooperation of work and study” ; compiled the first set of textbook of technical colleges in China; and first unified mechanical engineering nouns in China.

Mao Yisheng Bridge

茅以升桥

茅以升（1896—1989年），字唐臣，江苏镇江人，我国著名土木工程学家，桥梁专家，工程教育家，中国科学院院士，美国工程院院士、中央研究院院士。1928年12月至1930年7月，出任北洋工学院院长。抗日战争胜利后，茅以升再次被任命为国立北洋大学校长，因同时受命主持修复钱塘江大桥而未到校任职。

Mao Yisheng (1896-1989), also named as Tangchen, was born in Zhenjiang City of Jiangsu Province, a famous civil engineering scholar, bridge expert, engineering educator, academician of Chinese Academy of Sciences, member of US National Academy of Engineering, and academician of Academia Sinica. He has taken up the post of president of Peiyang Engineering College from December 1928 to July 1930. He has been appointed as the president of Peiyang University from 1946 to 1948. However, he hasn’ t accepted the post for the reason of repairing the Qiantang River bridge.

Mao Yisheng Bridge

张国藩桥

张国藩（1905—1975年），湖北安陆人，著名物理学家、力学家、教育家、国家一级教授。新中国刚成立时，张国藩实际主持北洋大学的学校工作，迅速地恢复了学校的教学秩序。1951年北洋大学由教育部定名为天津大学，张国藩任教授，历任副校长、校长，为天津大学的建设与发展历尽心血。

Zhang Guofan (1905-1975), was born in Anlu of Hubei, is a famous physicist, dynamicist, educator, and country-level professor. When PRC was just founded, Zhang Guofan directed school work actually, so the university' s teaching order was recovered rapidly. Peiyang University was renamed as Tianjin University by the Ministry of Education in 1952, and Zhang Guofan has served as professor, vice president and president, exerting his utmost efforts for the construction and development of Tianjin University.

Li Shusen Bridge

李曙森桥

李曙森（1910—1998年）河北霸县人。李曙森是我国杰出的教育家，在先后担任天津大学副校长、党委书记、校长、名誉校长期间，他以一个教育家的远见卓识积极探索新中国高等教育的规律，为天津大学和我国高等教育事业的发展作出了卓越贡献。1983年，他联名三位老教育家执笔《关于将50所左右高等院校列为国家重点建设项目的建议》上书中央，受到中央领导高度重视，催生了“211工程”和“985工程”。

Li Shusen (1910-1998), born in Ba County of Hebei Province, an outstanding educator in China. He has made remarkable contribution to Tianjin University and China' s higher education cause through positively exploring high education rules when he served as vice president, party secretary, president, and honorary president of Tianjin University. He and three other old educators submitted Suggestion on Listing about 50 Institutions of Higher Learning as State Key Construction Projects to the CPC Central Commitee in 1983, which was highly concerned by central leaders, thus promoting the birth of "Project 211" and "Project 985".

Three rings, six longitudinal roads and nine branch roads

三环六纵九支路

天津大学于2014年4月在全校和校友范围内启动了新校区主干道路征名活动，共征集到方案812份，道路名称5 000余个。在此基础上，学校组织专门力量，对新校区一期建设的113处道路、楼宇及景观进行了命名，并面向全校师生及有关单位、专家征求意见，结合广大师生意愿，反复求证，几经修改，形成了目前的命名方案。命名在体现北洋大学—天津大学悠久的历史和深厚的人文底蕴的同时，充分吸收了现代大学和中国传统文化中的育人理念，且考虑新老校区之间的情感和文脉延续，具有天津大学的特色和独创性。命名还注重其明确的方位指示等功能性作用，考虑相邻统一、顺序方向一致、一二期工程延续性等因素，使命名成体系、有规律。

In the April 2014, Tianjin University started main road naming activity for the new campus. Naming activity has been widely concerned by teachers, students, and schoolfellows since its commencement. We have collected 812 schemes and more than 5,000 road names. On this basis, the leading group organized special forces to name 113 roads, buildings, and landscapes in phase I of the new campus, seeking for opinions from all teachers and students, relevant units, and experts. The current naming scheme is formed with the combination of intentions of all teachers and students through several times of discussions and revisions. Naming embodies long history and profound humanistic connotations of Peiyang University—Tianjin University, fully absorbs education concepts of modern university and Chinese traditional culture, and considers emotion and cultural patrimony of the new and old campus, with features and originalities of Tianjin University. Naming pays attention to the specific direction indication functions, as well as adjacency and unification, the same order and direction, and duration of phase I and phase II project, so naming is systematic and organized.

Three rings

三环

内环：明德道　Inner Ring: Mingde Road

中环：亲民道　Middle Ring: Qinmin Road

外环：至善道　Outer Ring: Zhishan Road

三环语出我国传统典籍《大学》开篇：“大学之道，在明明德，在亲民，在止于至善。”意思是说，大学的宗旨在于弘扬光明正大的品德，在于使人弃旧图新，在于使人达到最完善的境界。

The names originated from the opening of *The Great Learning*, a traditional book in China. It means the purposes of “Great Learning” are to carry forward aboveboard morality, to let people reject the old for the new, and to make people achieve the most perfect realm.

Six longitudinal roads

六纵

兴学路 Xingxue Road

根据学校办学思想和不同历史时期的校址变迁或标志性事件命名，以天津大学“兴学强国”的办学使命开宗明义，通过学校建校以来的校址变迁（博文书院旧址、西沽校区、西北工学院旧址之一陕西城固县七星寺、卫津路校区以及津南新校区），纪念学校120年波澜壮阔的发展历程。

Such roads are named according to the ideas of running school and university site changes or iconic events in different historical periods. Tianjin University' s mission of "running school and making the state powerful" makes clear the purpose from the very beginning, in order to commemorate the university' s magnificent development history in the past 120 years through university site changes since the commencement (former site of Bowen Academy, Xigu Campus, Qixing Temple in Chenggu County of Shaanxi Province — a former site of Northwest Engineering College, Weijin Road Campus, and Jinnan New Campus).

博文路 Bowen Road

该命名来自于学校建校之初的首个校址。1895年10月2日，光绪皇帝御笔钦准，成立天津北洋西学学堂，校址在天津北运河畔大营门博文书院旧址，次年北洋西学学堂正式更名为北洋大学堂。

The name comes from the first school site of the university. Guangxu Emperor approved to establish Tianjin Peiyang Western Learning School on October 2nd, 1895, located in the former site of Bowen Academy, Daying Gate, Beiyun Riverside, Tianjin, and then Peiyang Western Learning School was formally renamed as Peiyang University in the next year.

西沽路 Xigu Road

该命名取材于北洋大学堂西沽校区。1900年，八国联军入侵津京，北洋大学堂校舍为敌兵所霸占，学校被迫停办。1903年4月，北洋大学堂在西沽正式复课。

The name comes from Xigu Campus of Peiyang University. The Eight-Power Allied Forces invaded Tianjin and Beijing in 1900, Peiyang University' s buildings were occupied by enemy soldiers, and the university was forced to be suspended. Beiyang University resumed classes in Xigu in April, 1903.

七星路 Qixing Road

该命名取材于西北工学院陕西城固七星寺旧址。抗日战争开始后，西北工学院时期的学生被安排到陕西城固县七星寺村上课，学生在七星寺村刻苦学习、弦歌不辍，伴随学生读书的灯火夜夜长明，被称为“七星灯火”。

It comes from Qixing Temple in Chenggu County of Shaanxi Province — a former site of Northwest Engineering College. Students of Northwest Engineering College, were arranged to Qixing Temple to have classes. Students studied hard and lights were bright on every night, so it was called as "seven-day lights".

双台路 Shuangtai Road

该命名取材于目前天津大学卫津路校区地址，即“六里台”和“七里台”。多年来，这“两个里台”已然成为广大师生和校友心中情系母校的重要符号。

The name comes from the sites of Weijin Road Campus of Tianjin University, namely “Liuli Tai” and “Qili Tai”. Over the years, such two places have become important symbols for teachers, students, and schoolfellows to memory the Vniversity.

新元路 Xinyuan Road

2015年天津大学津南新校区投入使用，适逢学校喜迎120年华诞，以“新元”命名，寓意为全校师生站在新的历史起点，“圆梦新校区，起航新甲子，开启新纪元”。

Jinnan New Campus of Tianjin University came into service in 2015, meeting the 120th anniversary of the university, so it is named as “Xinyuan”, meaning all teachers and students will stand on the new historical starting point. “Fulfilling dreams in the new campus, beginning a new 60-year circle, and starting a new era.”

Nine branch roads

九支路

侯德榜路 Hou Debang Road

该道路邻近化工教学组团，故以曾在北洋大学任教的我国著名化学家侯德榜先生命名。

The road is close to Chemical Engineering Teaching Group, so it is named after Mr. Hou Debang, a famous chemist, who has worked as a teacher in Peiyang University.

敬业路 Jingye Road

该道路邻近行政服务中心，故命名为“敬业路”，寓意为激励全校教职员工爱岗敬业、服务奉献。

The road is close to Administrative Service Center, so it is named as “Jingye Road”, to stimulate the faculty to work wholeheartedly for the university.

王正廷道 Wang Zhengting Road

该道路邻近体育公园，以北洋大学杰出校友、我国著名外交家、“中国奥林匹克之父”王正廷先生命名。

The road is close to Sports Park, so it is named after Mr. Wang Zhengting, an outstanding alumnus of Peiyang University, a famous diplomatist in China, and “the father of Chinese Olympics”.

花堤道　Huadi Road

该命名取自校歌中 “花堤蔼蔼”，契合了道路邻近的湖畔两岸分别遍种桃花和海棠的实际景观。

“Huadi Road” comes from “flower banks” in the lines of school song. In addition, peach blossoms and cherry-apple trees are blossoming on the banks nearby.

英华道　Yinghua Road

该命名取自校歌中 “英华卓荦”，同花堤道一样，契合道路邻近的湖畔两岸分别遍种桃花和海棠的实际景观。

“Yinghua Road” comes from “outstanding talents” in the lines of school song, the same to the “Huadi Road”, peach blossoms and cherry-apple trees are blossoming on the banks nearby.

书田南道 / 书田北道　South Shutian Road/North Shutian Road

因位于书田广场南北两侧，故命名为“书田南道”和“书田北道”。

These two roads are located on south and north sides of Shutian Square, so they are named as “South Shutian Road” and “North Shutian Road”.

求是南道 / 求是北道　South Qiushi Road/North Qiushi Road

因位于求是大道南北两侧，故命名为“求是南道”和“求是北道”。

These two roads are located on south and north sides of Qiushi Road, so they are named as “South Qiushi Road” and “North Qiushi Road”.

公共建筑

Public Building

Main Building （31-33#）

主楼（31~33 楼）

设计者：崔愷、任祖华、叶水清、梁丰、彭彦、曹洋

Designers: Cui Kai, Ren Zuhua, Ye Shuiqing, Liang Feng, Peng Yan, Cao Yang

以圆形体量化解轴线转折的矛盾。校园的入口空间的轴线与核心岛的轴线在项目用地的中部形成转折，因此我们在轴线转折处设计了圆形的体量，形成自然的转折，化解了轴线转折的矛盾。

开放化的校园空间体系。整组建筑以圆形的广场为中心，建筑沿广场周边布置，呈现出一种开放的姿态。圆形广场与东侧的校前广场和西侧的核心岛步行空间共同形成开放化的校园空间体系。

“圆”与“方”的呼应。在校园主轴线上，校前区主楼建筑和图书馆建筑是两个重要的节点。圆形的主楼与方形的图书馆在空间上形成了遥相呼应的形态。

建筑个性的表达。建筑的造型与不同的功能相统一。文科组团多层次的院落和坡屋顶的造型源自传统的书院空间，理科和材料组团空间则体现出现代理性主义的特点。

Defusing contradictions of axis transition with the use of round mass. Axis at the entrance of the campus and the axis of core island form transition in the middle of the project land. Therefore, we set a round mass in the turning place of axis to form a natural turning point and to defuse contradictions of axis transition.

Open campus space system. The whole group of buildings takes the round square as the center and buildings are arranged along the square, showing a kind of opening posture. The round square, the square on the east side and the core island on the west side form the open space system.

Echo of “round” and “square”. In the principal axis of the campus, Main Building and Library Building are two important nodes. Round Main Building and square Library echo each other in space.

Expression of building individuality. Architectural modeling unifies different functions. The modeling of multi-layered courtyards and sloping-roof of Arts Group comes from traditional Academy space, while Science and Material Group space embodies features of modern rationality.

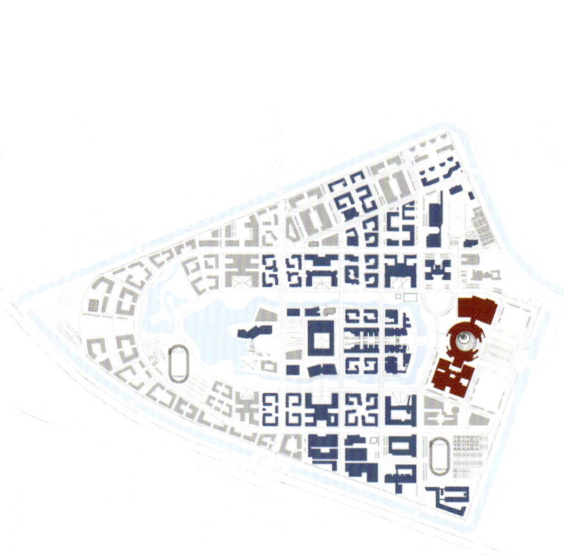
区位图

为体现学校新老校区之间的传承性，新校区教学组团建筑亦以数字排序，并根据卫津路校区楼号接续排列。出于为卫津路校区未来建设预留空间考虑，新校区楼号自“第31教学楼”为始，并按照由南至北的顺时针顺序依次命名。主楼北配楼、主楼和主楼南配楼分别为第31教学楼、第32教学楼和第33教学楼。

In order to reflect inheritance of the new and old campus, teaching buildings in the new campus are ordered in numbers, following the number of Weijin Road Campus. In consideration of reserving space for future construction of Weijin Road Campus, the building number of the new campus starts from "the 31st teaching building", and they are named in clockwise order. The North Skirt Building and South Skirt Building to Main Building and Main Building are the 31st, 32nd and 33st Teaching Building respectively.

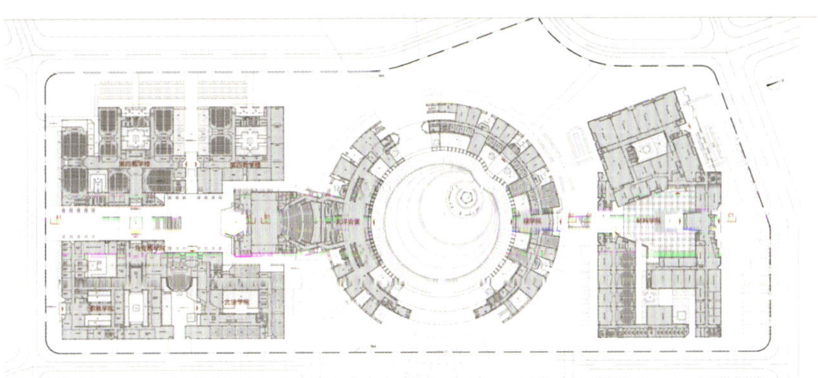

首层平面图

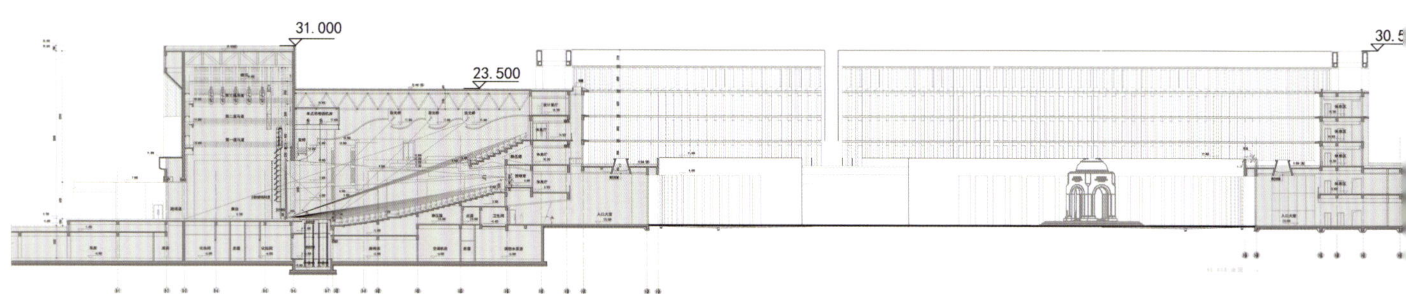

剖面图

剖面图

入口大堂效果图

Comprehensive Experiment Building (47-49#)

综合实验楼(47~49 楼)

设计者：崔愷、任祖华、梁丰、朱巍、李欣

Designers: Cui Kai, Ren Zuhua, Liang Feng, Zhu Wei, Li Xin

项目位于新校区核心岛的最前端，东西主轴线从建筑之间穿过。整个建筑由物理教学实验中心、电气电子教学实验中心和语音教室、计算机教学实验中心3个建筑单体组成。

设计中我们严格按照总体规划设定的建筑贴线要求布置建筑，以求形成整体的校园空间环境。通过形体的切分，尽量削减建筑的体量，形成适宜的尺度。建筑的外侧形成层层的平台，一方面使建筑与周边的绿化空间、水体空间建立起了对话关系；另一方面，一系列的退台空间也为学生提供了多层次的室外开放交流空间。建筑造型从功能出发，力求简洁朴素，体现教育建筑的自身特色，仅对主轴线两侧的两个入口空间做了特殊的处理，形成进入核心岛的两个标志点。

The project is located in the most significant end of the new campus's core island. The principal axis from east to west passed through the building. The whole building is made up of Physics Teaching Laboratory Center, Electric & Electronic Teaching Experimental Center and Language Classroom, and Computer Teaching and Experiment Test Center.

In the design, we arrange the buildings strictly according to building line requirements set by overall planning, so as to form integral space. It cuts down building mass as possible through body cut to form suitable size. The out layer of the building forms layer-upon-layer platform. On one hand, it builds up dialogic relationship with surrounding green space and water space, on the other hand, it provides multi-layered outdoor open exchange space for students by a series of set-back space. Architectural modeling starts from functions, strives for conciseness and simplicity, embodies features of educational building, and conducts special dealing towards two entrance spaces on both sides of principal axis, to form two mark points of core island.

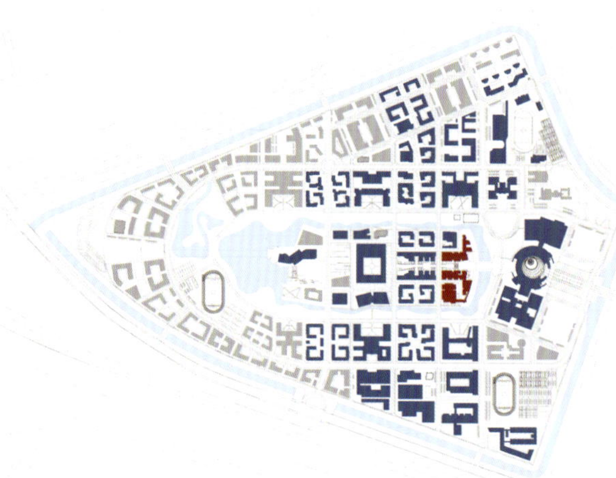

区位图

综合实验楼的3个单体建筑在编入序号统一命名的同时，分别命名为静算楼（第47教学楼）、规圆楼（第48教学楼）和矩方楼（第49教学楼）。静算，出自《晋书·殷浩传》，其含义为“审慎地规划”。规圆矩方，出自《汉书·律历志上》，含义为“够标准、合法度”。以静算、规圆和矩方命名3座实验楼，不仅与其建筑各自的外观和用途贴合，也旨在突出天大师生秉承实事求是的校风和严谨治学的优良传统。

The three units of Comprehensive Experiment Building were named as Jingsuan Building (The 47th Teaching Building) ,Guiyuan Building (The 48th Teaching Building) and Jufang Building (The 49th Teaching Building) respectively. Jingsuan means planning carefully. Guiyuan means being standard. Jufang means being legal. Names of such three comprehensive experiment buildings not only fit for buildings' appearance and usage but also aim to highlight the inheritance of Tianjin University's teachers and students for the concept "seeking truth from facts" and the solid studying tradition of the university.

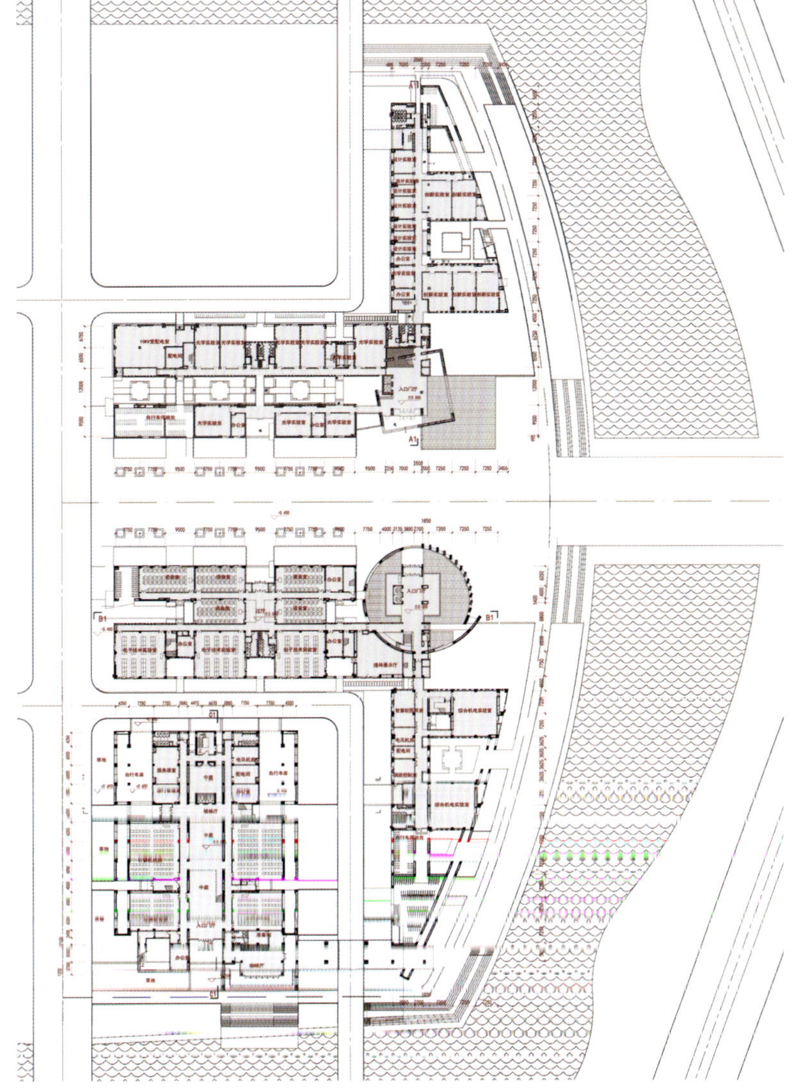

首层平面图

Library and Information and Network Center

图书馆及信网中心

设计者:周恺、张莉兰、吴岳、章宁、王力新、李博、刘若谷、左克伟、郭恩健、封新华、安君、曹睿智、刘鑫、李江

Designers: Zhou Kai, Zhang Lilan, Wu Yue, Zhang Ning, Wang Lixin, Li Bo, Liu Ruogu, Zuo Kewei, Guo Enjian, Feng Xinhua, An Jun, Cao Ruizhi, Liu Xin, Li Jiang

图书馆

图书馆处于新校区的中心位置，建筑主体重心与校园东西轴线相重合，周边有公共教学区环绕，是各个景观轴线交汇处。图书馆总体借鉴中国传统建筑的以“庭院”为中心的空间模式，营造一个具有现代校园精神的公共性、开放性的文化场所。建筑总体呈长方形，中部设有72 m×72 m的室外庭院（中心庭院），并以158 m×117 m的空间体量，以玻璃、铝幕墙为主的通透明快、水平伸展的形体表现了其现代、开放的气质。

总体布局注重体现现代大学多样化的功能需要。由中部贯通东西的空间入口，引导人流进入中心庭院空间，再依次到达图书馆大厅、学术报告厅、多功能厅、自习教室、书店、咖啡茶吧等功能空间，同时，庭院空间也提供了优雅静谧的环境和室外阅读休憩的场所，在此也可举办各种典礼仪式和文化活动。

总体布局也充分融入了绿色建筑的理念，结合平面功能和室内外庭园布置，最大限度利用自然采光和自然通风。建筑以最大的周边布置阅览空间，提供足够的自然光照度，并通过阅览空间相对的外墙开窗和内外庭院、天井等组织自然通风。另外，在选材细节上也注重强化建筑的地域性、文化性，结合现代建筑特色、生态环保，在创造出一个物质资源空间载体的同时，也突出了其校园生活核心空间和精神场所空间的作用。

Library

Library is located in the center of the new campus and the gravity center for major structure of the building and axis from east to west interlace, with public teaching area around, which is the intersection of landscape axes. Generally, the library builds a public and open culture place with modern campus spirit through referring to “courtyard-centered” spatial pattern of Chinese traditional building. It is a rectangle, with a 72 m×72 m exterior courtyard (central courtyard) in the middle. With 158 m×117 m spatial mass, horizontal extension, and glass and aluminum curtain wall, the building is modern and open.

Overall layout pays attention to embodying diversified function requirements of modern university. Entry from the space cuts through east and west in the center and guides people into central courtyard and to such functional spaces as Library Hall, Academic Hall, Multi-functional Hall, Study Room, Book Store, Coffee, and Tea Bar. And at the same time, the courtyard space also provides elegant and quiet places for outdoor reading and rest, where students can hold various ceremonies and cultural activities.

The overall layout blends in the concept of green building, which uses natural lighting and natural ventilation to a great extent with the combination of plane function and interior and exterior courtyard layout. The building sets reading space with the largest rim, provides enough natural illumination, and organizes natural ventilation through exterior-wall window, interior and exterior courtyard, and patio. In addition, it pays attention to intensifying buildings' regionalism and culture in material selection and details. It stands out core space and spirit place of its campus life while creating a material resource space carrier, with the combination of features of modern buildings and ecological environmental protection.

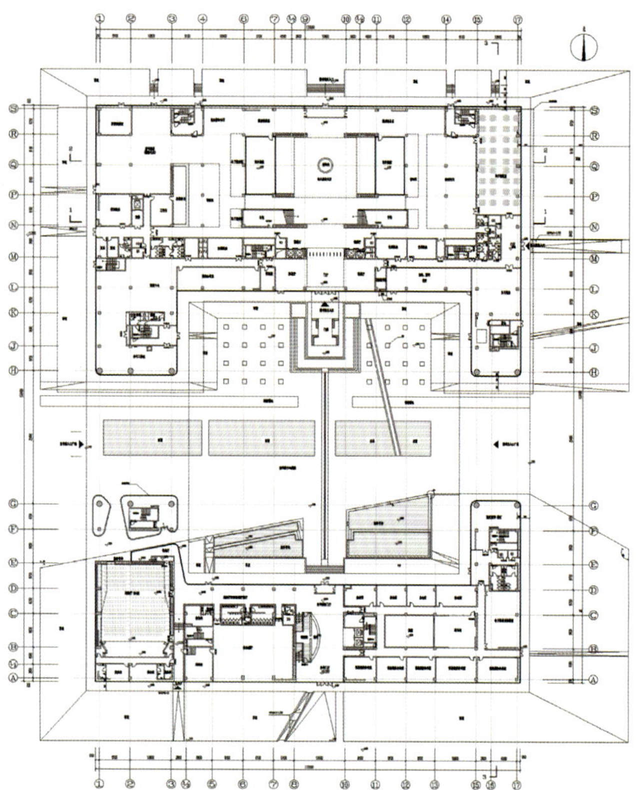
首层平面图

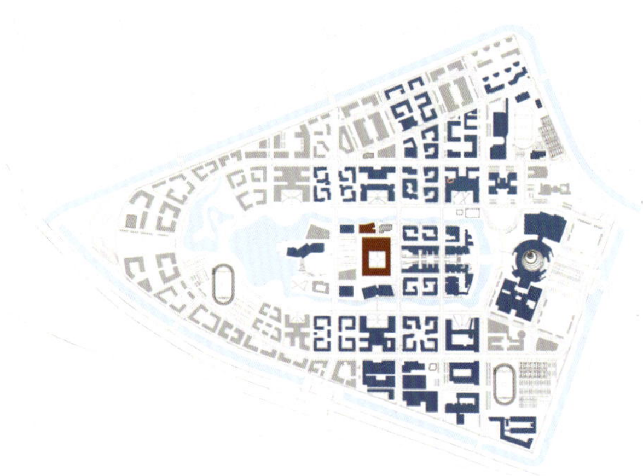
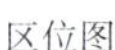
区位图

天窗
3000
空调机房
货梯
工作间
电子检索区
存包
公共服务大厅
陈展空间
卫生间
RD
QD
-5.400
汽车库
直饮水机房

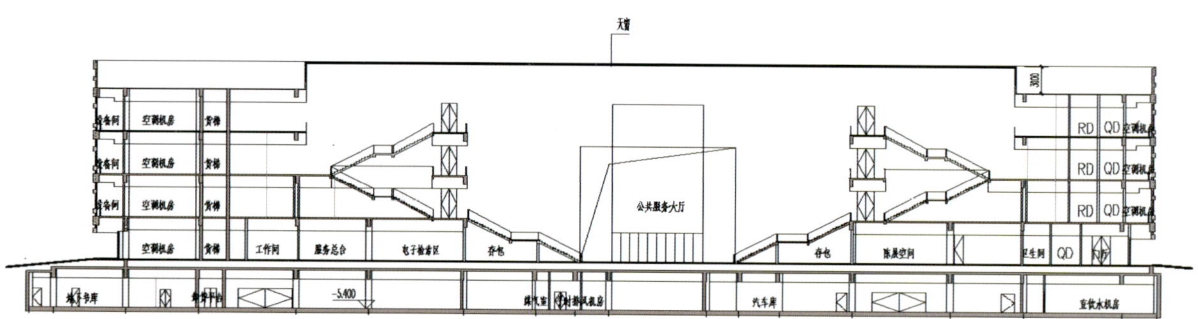

剖面图

TIANJIN UNIVERSITY LIBARY
天津大学图书馆
1895-2015

D2-P09

信网中心

图书馆北侧为其所属的信网中心，与图书馆隔路沿街布置，主要出入口位于东侧，也采用庭院式布置解决采光、通风问题。因其功能专业性的要求，外形相对图书馆处理得较为封闭，但通过外檐凹凸变化和材料质感有别于图书馆的处理，具有独特的外部形象。信网中心东侧结合景观绿化布置集中自行车停车场，另设地下车库汽车坡道，作为地下车库主要出入口连接校十路。图书馆西侧隔路为绿化景观广场，因功能所需另行布置了地下车库坡道出口，此地下车库出口作为运输、后勤保障和紧急疏散之用。

Information and Network Center

The Information and Network Center is in the north side of the library. The main entrance is located in the east side, which solves the issue of lighting and ventilation with the use of courtyard layout. Compared with library, it is relatively closed for requirements in functional specialty. However, it has unique exterior image. Bicycle parking lot is located in the east side and car ramp of underground garage is set as the main entrance of underground garage. Green landscape square is located in the other side of the road of library and ramp entrance of underground garage is set separately, used for transportation, logistical support, and urgent evacuation.

The First Public Teaching Building（44#）

第一公共教学楼（44 楼）

设计者:周恺、吴岳、章宁、王力新、鹏帆、安君、曹睿智、刘鑫

Designers: Zhou Kai, Wu Yue, Zhang Ning, Wang Lixin, Peng Fan, An Jun, Cao Ruizhi, Liu Xin

第一公共教学楼处于新校区图书馆南侧，建筑主体轴线与图书馆南北轴线重合，毗邻宿舍区，南侧有景观河流，位置重要，景观良好。建筑以两个互成15度角的体量呼应南侧河岸，并形成西南向主入口，同时借鉴中国传统建筑 “庭院” 的空间布置模式，营造了一个具有现代校园精神的教学场所。

建筑由两组单侧走廊的教学单元围合成一个室外庭院，两个教学单元内部各自围绕室内中庭安排功能。建筑外形完整、简洁，建筑东西长130m，以砖、玻璃为主的建筑材料表现了其现代、简洁、高效的校园气质。总体布局注重体现教学楼的特点，考虑新校区的人流方向，将主入口分别置于建筑东西两侧，并充分考虑到与图书馆南侧入口的贯通，架空空间成为次入口，并成为了教学楼空间的一大亮点。同时，教学楼内设计的庭院空间也提供了优雅、静谧的环境和室外阅读休憩的场所。

第一公共教学楼作为天津大学新校区三星绿色建筑的示范工程，在建筑方案阶段就与绿色建筑的要求相结合，将教室均做单侧走廊布置，最大限度利用自然采光和自然通风，同时也和教学楼内的3个庭院形成良好的互动，形成优质的教学空间。另外，在选材细节上也注重强化建筑的地域性、文化性，一方面运用砖作为主要建筑材料与天津大学的整体气质相匹配，另一方面，采用当代的建筑语言处理砖材料，形成文化气质与现代气质并重的教学建筑。

The First Public Teaching Building is in the south side of library of the new campus and its principal axis and north and south axis of library are in line. It adjoins dormitory area, with landscape river in the south, of important location and favorable landscape. The building echoes river bank in the south side with two masses with 15° angle, forming the main entry door of southwest direction. And at the same time, referring to spatial arrangement mode of Chinese traditional "courtyard", it creates a teaching site with modern campus spirit.

Two groups of teaching units with one-sided corridor form an exterior courtyard. Architectural appearance is complete and concise, which is 130m in length from east to west. In addition, building materials giving priority to bricks and glass express its campus temperament of modern times, conciseness, and efficiency. As for overall layout, designers pay attention to features of the teaching building, considering people stream direction of new campus, to set main entrance on the east and west side of the building, and take full account of cutting through south entrance of the library to regard the empty space as the next entrance. And at the same time, courtyard space designed in the teaching building also provides elegant and quiet environment and exterior rest and reading.

As a demonstration project of three-star green building on the new campus of Tianjin University, it combines requirements of green building in building scheme stage and utilizes natural lighting and natural ventilation to a great extent. And at the same time, it forms a favorable interaction with three courtyards in the teaching building, to have superior teaching space. In addition, it focuses on intensifying regionalism and culturing of building in details of material selection. On one hand, bricks are the main building materials which match with overall temperament of Tianjin University; on the other hand, brick materials are handled with the use of contemporary architectural language, to form a teaching building laying equal stress on cultural ethos and modern characters.

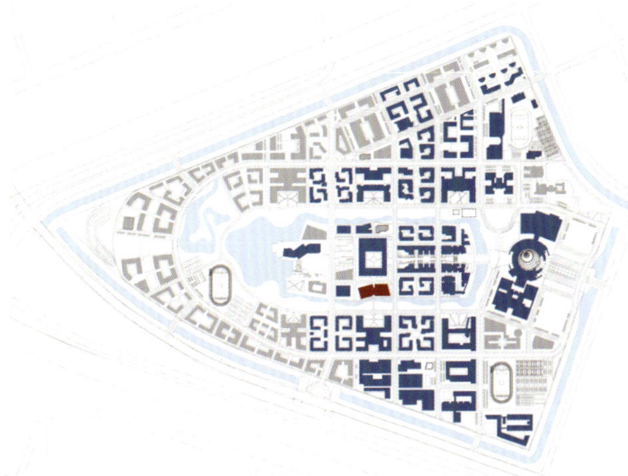

区位图

The Second Public Teaching Building (45、46#)

第二公共教学楼（45和46楼）

设计者：郑权、籍成科、张宇、王征、王海、王一丰、张柳娟、赵晨、卢燃、林琳、胡思捷等

Designers: Zheng Quan, Ji Chengke, Zhang Yu, Wang Zheng, Wang Hai, Wang Yifeng, Zhang Liujuan, Zhao Chen, Lu Ran, Lin Lin, Hu Sijie, etc.

第二公共教学楼位于新校区中轴线的中段，共占4个地块，建筑分南北两栋，各4层。设计中将南侧两个地块与北侧两个地块通过过街楼两两相连，使建筑形态更为舒展，强化中轴线两侧的序列感；形体与两侧的图书馆与综合实验楼相呼应，并采用比较低调的设计手法，使建筑成为中轴线两端重要建筑的背景，形成整体和谐的环境关系。外墙材料为页岩砖，设计方案根据页岩砖的尺寸和工艺要求使用严格的平面及立面模数，并采用砖损耗较少的砌筑方法，在实现严谨的立面效果的同时提高经济性。

建筑功能以公共教室为主，设计上尽量采用单廊布置教室，提供良好的采光和通风条件。教室的墙体和吊顶按声学设计要求采用不同的声学处理材料，以提高教学中的声学表现。在外窗加设反光遮阳板改善教室窗口与教室深处的照度均匀度，并尽量减少白天人工照明的使用，以节约能源。宽敞明亮的走廊和公共空间、舒适的教室，将为学生们提供宜人的学习环境。

The Second Public Teaching Building is located in the middle of central axis of the new campus, occupying four blocks in all and including south and north 4-storey buildings. Two blocks in the south and two blocks in the north are linked through bridge gallery, so that architectural form is more stretched, which can intensify sequence sense on both sides of central axis. The mass echoes with library and comprehensive experiment building on the two sides. Furthermore, low-key design method is adopted to form important building background on both sides of central axis and harmonious environment relations. External wall materials are shale bricks. As for design scheme, strict plane and facade modules are used in accordance with size and technological requirements of shale bricks and the brick laying method with less loss is used, to realize rigorous facade results and raise economy.

As for building function, designers attach most importance to public classrooms, adopting single corridor to fix up classroom and providing favorable lighting and atmospheric conditions. As for classrooms' wall and ceiling, different acoustic treatment materials are taken as per acoustic design requirements, as to enhance acoustics expressions in teaching. Adding light-reflecting sun louver can improve uniformity of illumination in classroom windows and deep places. It should also reduce application of artificial lighting as possible to save energy. Large and bright corridor and public space and comfortable classroom will offer pleasant learning environment for students.

区位图

45

1
2
3
4
5
6
7
8
9
10
11
12
13
14
A
B
C
1：主入口 4：门厅 7：弱点分机房 10：变配电室 13：休息厅
2：次入口 5：走廊 8：值班 11：消防控制室 14：智慧校园机房
3：教室 6：通道 9：自行车停车 12：库房

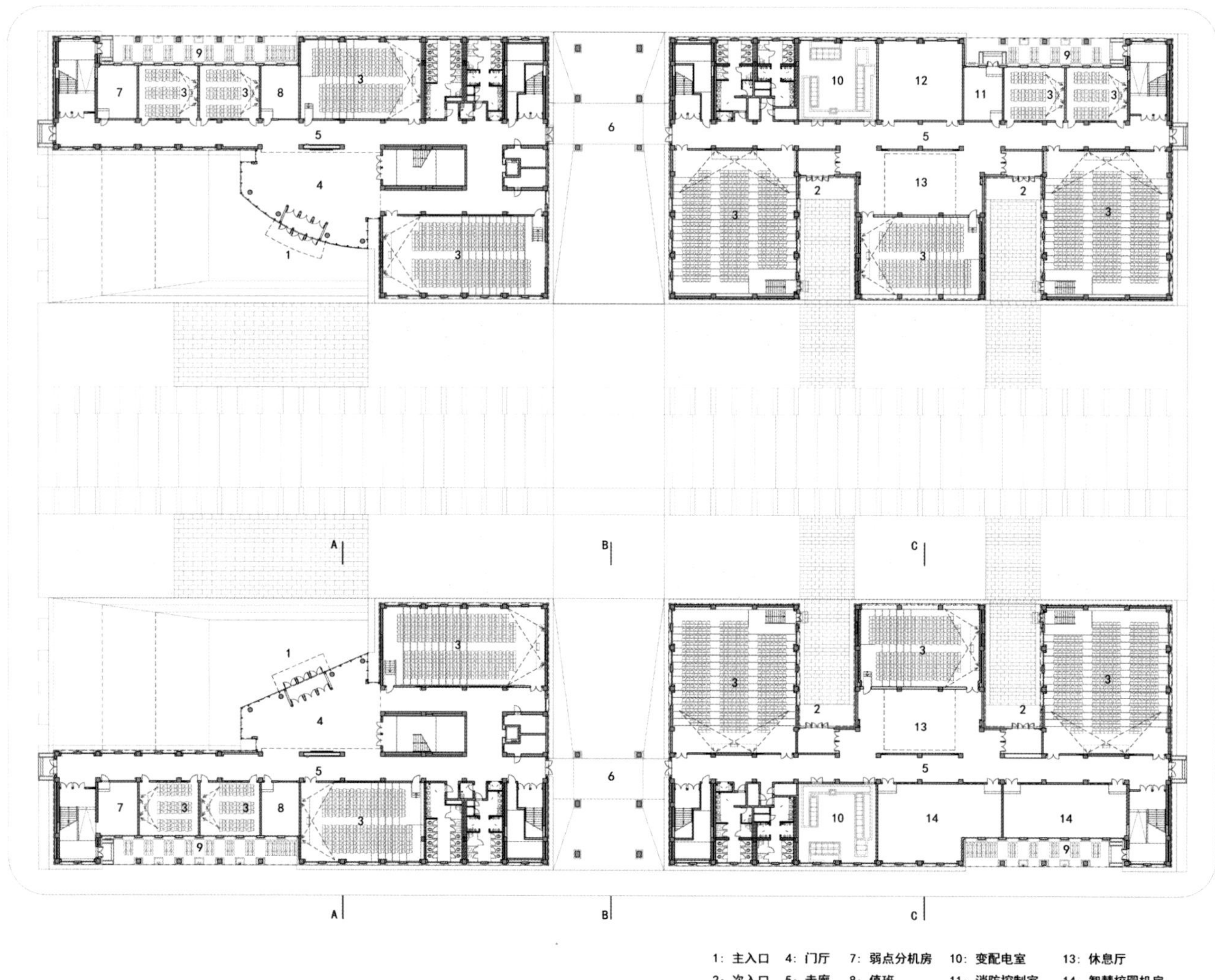

首层平面图

45

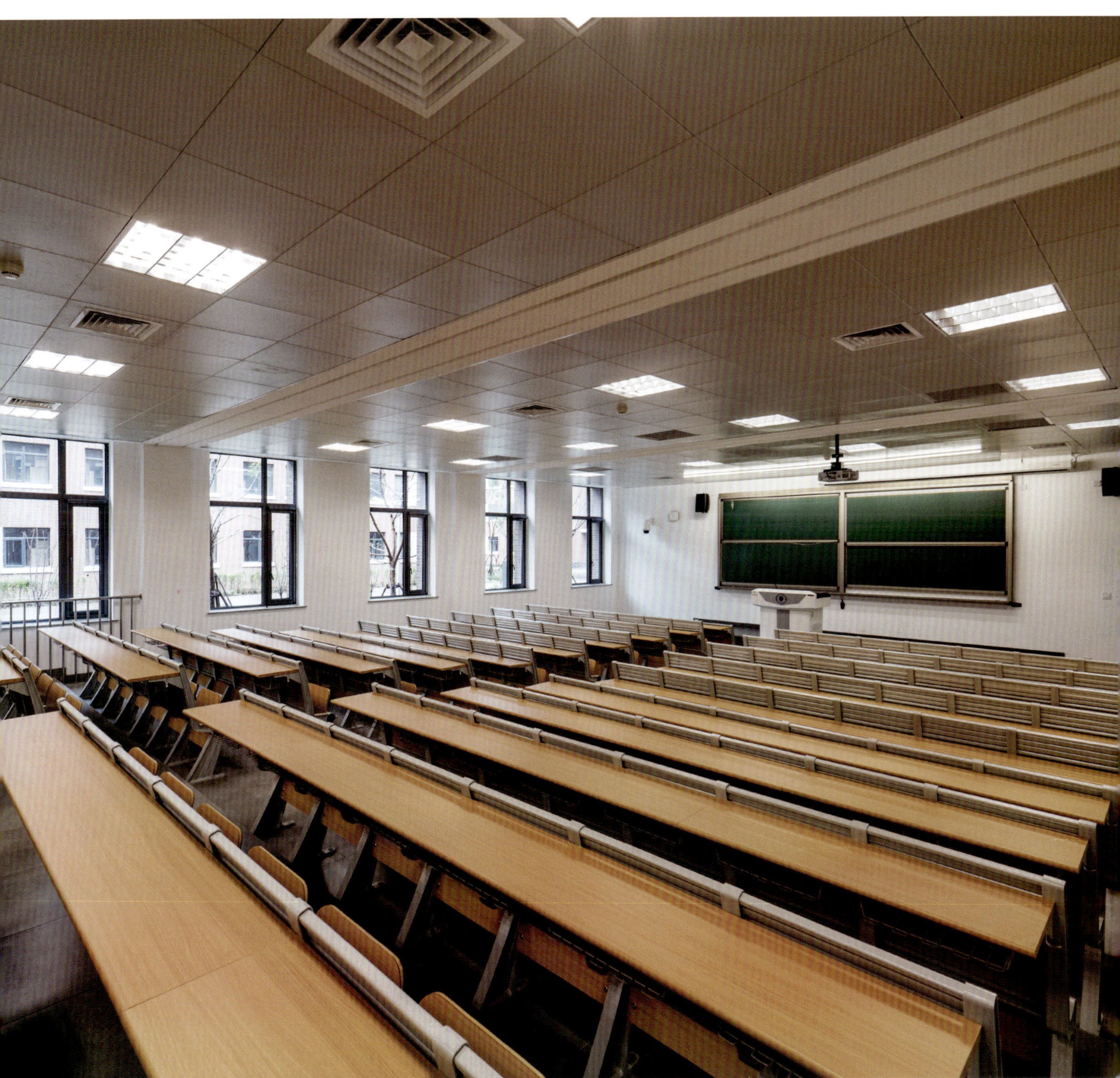

Student Center

学生中心

设计者:齐欣、刘阳、戴博军、于向东

Designers: Qi Xin, Liu Yang, Dai Bojun, Yu Xiangdong

学生中心坐落在新校园主轴线的尽端，突出水面的半岛将其引向开阔的自然景观，与轴线序列空间中端庄的校园景象形成对比。在这块东西长、南北窄的地段上，3个简单的矩形体块依次排开：从与教学中心区的严整对位，逐渐过渡到湖区的自由舒展。

校区这边，建筑的外墙沿用了校园通用的红砖，窗洞规律、严谨；湖区一侧，建筑的外墙变得通透，将优美的景色纳入其中；中间的一个房子承上启下，具有反射特质的外墙材料一边朦胧地反射着红色的砖墙，一边映照着透明的玻璃，同时，它还在反射着广场上的雕塑、湖区里的绿植和多变的天色。到了建筑的第3层，一条延续而蜿蜒的曲线将3个单体聚拢到了一起。蜿蜒间，柔形体的底面撑开了建筑入口的雨棚，它的侧面由穿孔金属板遮盖着，半透明板材后的房屋或院落若隐若现。恍惚间，直线与弧线的关系变得模糊：不知是平面演绎出了曲面，还是曲面滋生出了平面？不知是一栋建筑，还是三个房屋？

整栋建筑的设计从功能入手，让有限的面积产生最大的效益。它的造型，既考虑了与校园风格的协调，又结合了湖区的自然景致；既体现了天津大学严谨的校风，又描绘了年轻人的活泼，乃至浪漫。

Student Center is located in the end of principal axis of the new campus, which is brought to wide natural landscape by peninsula in the water, in contrast with elegant campus scene in the sequence space of axis. In the plot which is long from east to west while narrow from south to north, three simple rectangles are arranged successively: transitting from neat counterpoint of teaching center to freedom stretch of lake region.

The facade close to main campus uses red bricks which are usual in campus and window apertures are disciplinary and rigorous; the facade close to lake region is transparent, which brings beautiful scenery into the interior space; the middle house is a connecting link between the preceding and the following. Exterior wall materials with reflection characteristics reflect red brick walls faintly and shine upon transparent glass, echoing sculptures on the square, green plants in lake region, and versatile weather. In the 3/F of the building, a continuous and winding curve gathers three monomers. Underside of flexible body shoves off rain-shed of building entrance, whose side face is covered by perforated metal. Houses or courtyards behind semi-transparent panels are partly hidden and partly visible. The relationship between straight lines and arc becomes blurred: we don' t know whether planes deduce curved surfaces or curved surfaces breed planes? We don' t know whether there is a building or three rooms?

Design of the whole building starts from functions so that the limited area can generate the maximum benefits; its modeling considers coordination with campus style and combines natural landscape of lake region; it not only reflects rigorous school spirit of Tianjin University, but also describes liveness and even romance of young people.

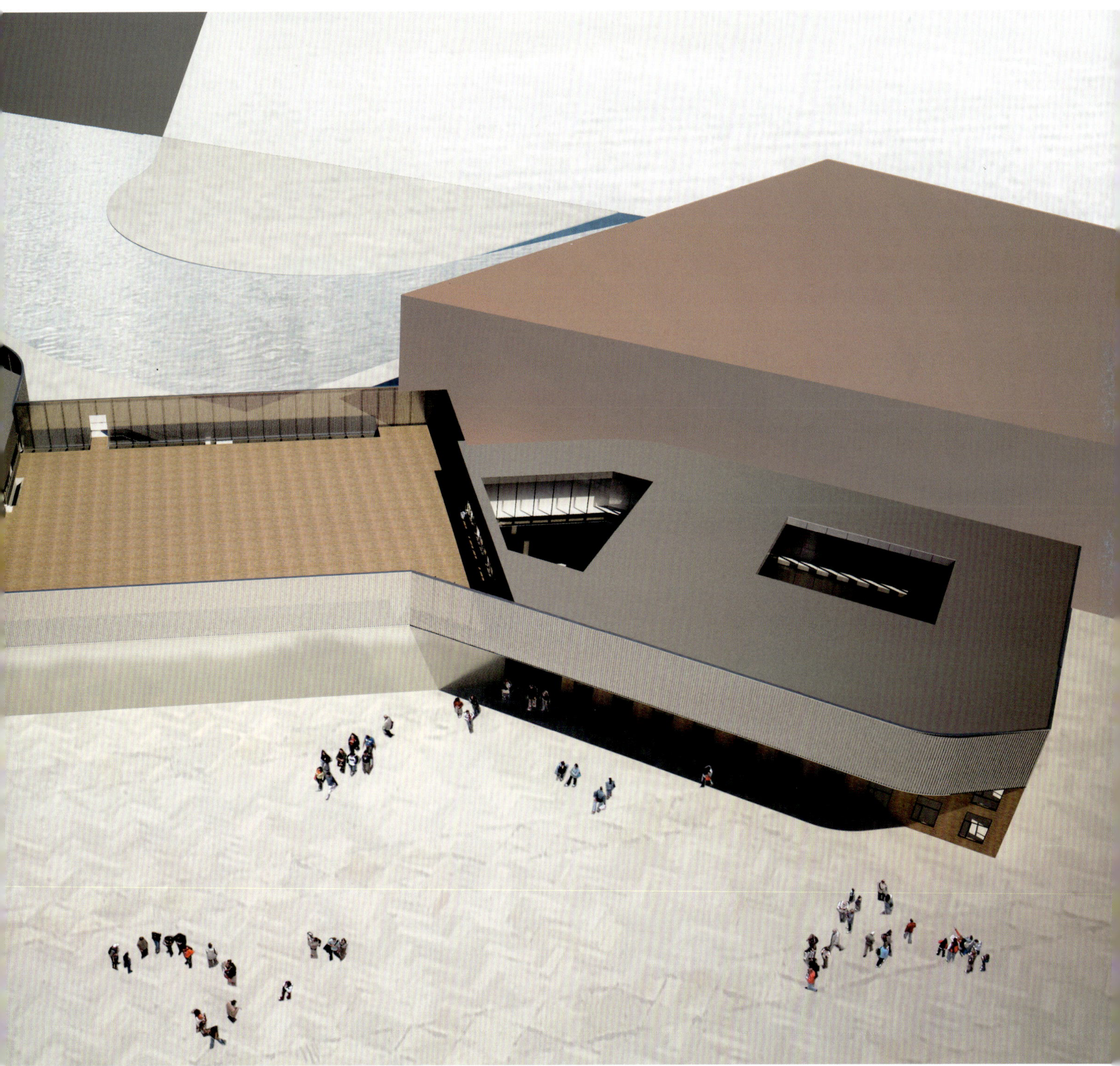

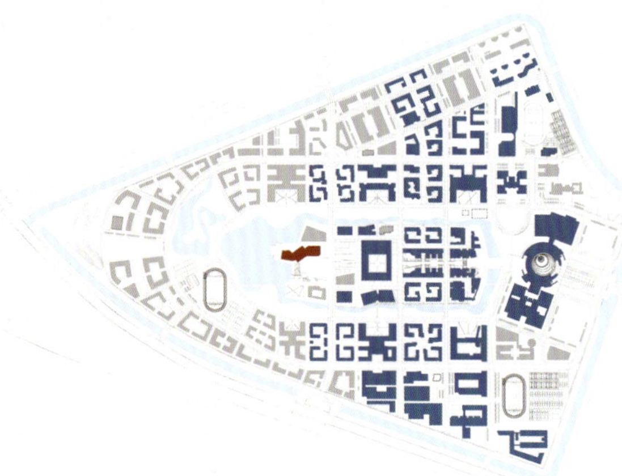

区位图

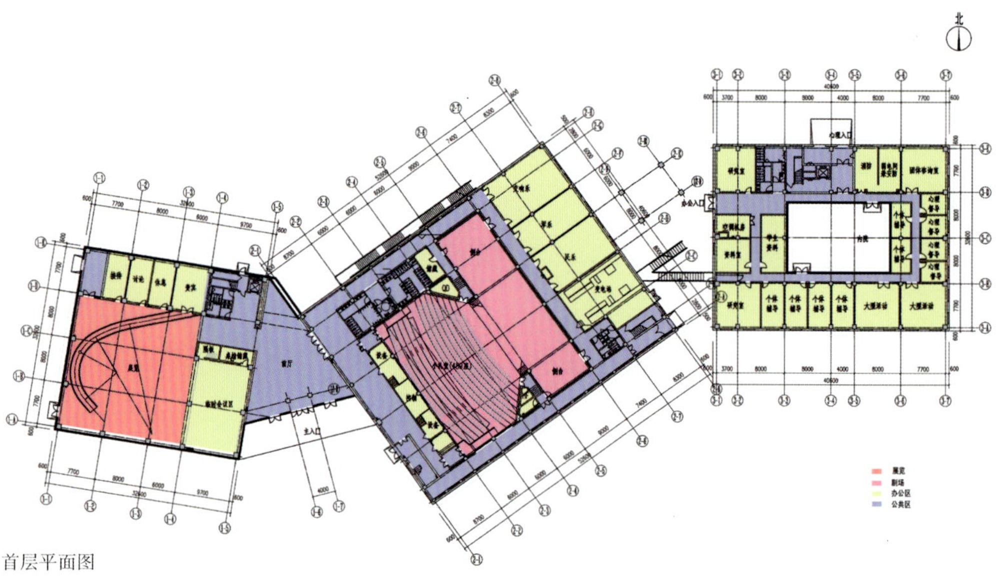

首层平面图

Administrative Service Center

行政服务中心

设计者:荆子洋、张键

Designers: Jing Ziyang, Zhang Jian

新校区行政服务中心设计力争体现天津大学百年老校的悠久底蕴及标志性时代特征。将多重院落嵌入建筑之中，尺度亲切，室内外空间丰富，模块化的功能分区有利于多功能合理布局，“化整为零”的体量创造良好的采光与通风条件，将自然院落融入办公环境。

引入“柱林”的概念，喻“十年树木，百年树人”，赋予建筑仪式感和标志性，前庭缓冲空间烘托了独特的建筑氛围。4层交通串联汇聚于景观楼梯，行走的人流结合顶部天窗的光影变换，获得步移景变的空间体验。从行政服务中心前开阔的广场经过柱廊、前庭进入门厅，通过景观楼梯到达茶歇及各办公区域，形成独具特色的空间序列。

Design for Administrative Service Center of the new campus strives for reflecting long-standing inside and iconic characteristics of the times of Tianjin University as an old university for over one hundred years. It implants multiple courtyards, with cordial scale and rich indoor and outdoor spaces. Modularized functional division is in favor of multi-functional rational distribution. The mass formed by "breaking the whole into parts" creates favorable lighting and ventilation conditions and blends natural courtyard into office environment.

It brings the concept of "pillar forest", which means "it takes ten years to grow trees but a hundred to cultivate people", endowing the buildings with ceremonial sense and landmark property. Front cushion space creates unique building atmosphere. Four-layer transportation gathers in landscape stairs. With the combination of shadow conversion of skylights on the top, stream of walking people can acquire spatial experiences of shifting scene changes. People enter into the entrance hall from the open square in front of Administrative Service Center, arriving at tea break and office areas through landscape stairs, which forms unique spatial sequence.

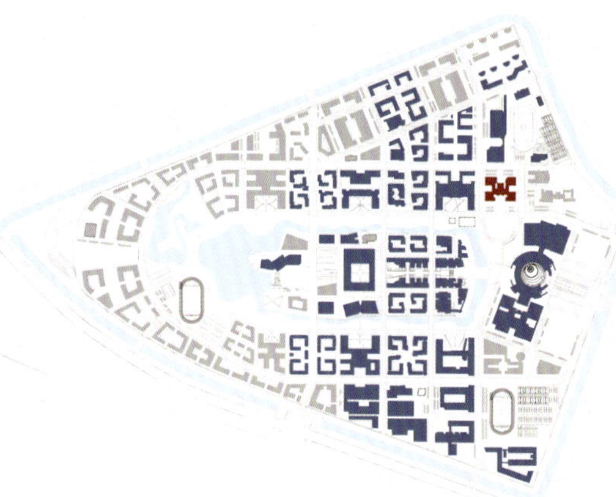

区位图

1A:1102m²
1C:1043m²
1B-1:3890m²
防火分区示意图
教工、学生服务区 613M²
其中
服务大厅 541M²
办公 72M²
财政办公区 1019M²
其中
财政大厅 715M²
会议室 65M²
办公 127M²
中层干部会议室:1间
面积:371M²
座位数 154个
通用办公室:15间
合标准办公室(36M²):25间
会议室:2间
面积 110M²
职工之家(含更衣室):
面积 224M²
综合接待室:1间
面积 110M²
贵宾室:1间
面积 62M²
信访办公:1间
面积 69M²
茶歇室:2间
面积 156M²
公共卫生间:3间
面积 146M²
设备用房
招标办公室
职工之家
会议
招生咨询办公室
录取办公室
空调机房
茶歇室
贵宾室
综合接待室
服务台
通高大厅
休息区
传达室
打印室
财务办公
中层干部会议室
371M²
座位数154
同声传译室
设备用房
办公
网络控制室
弱电间
安防及消防控制室
信访办公
机房
柜台
复核
财务大厅
715M²
教工、学生服务大厅
541M²
首层平面图

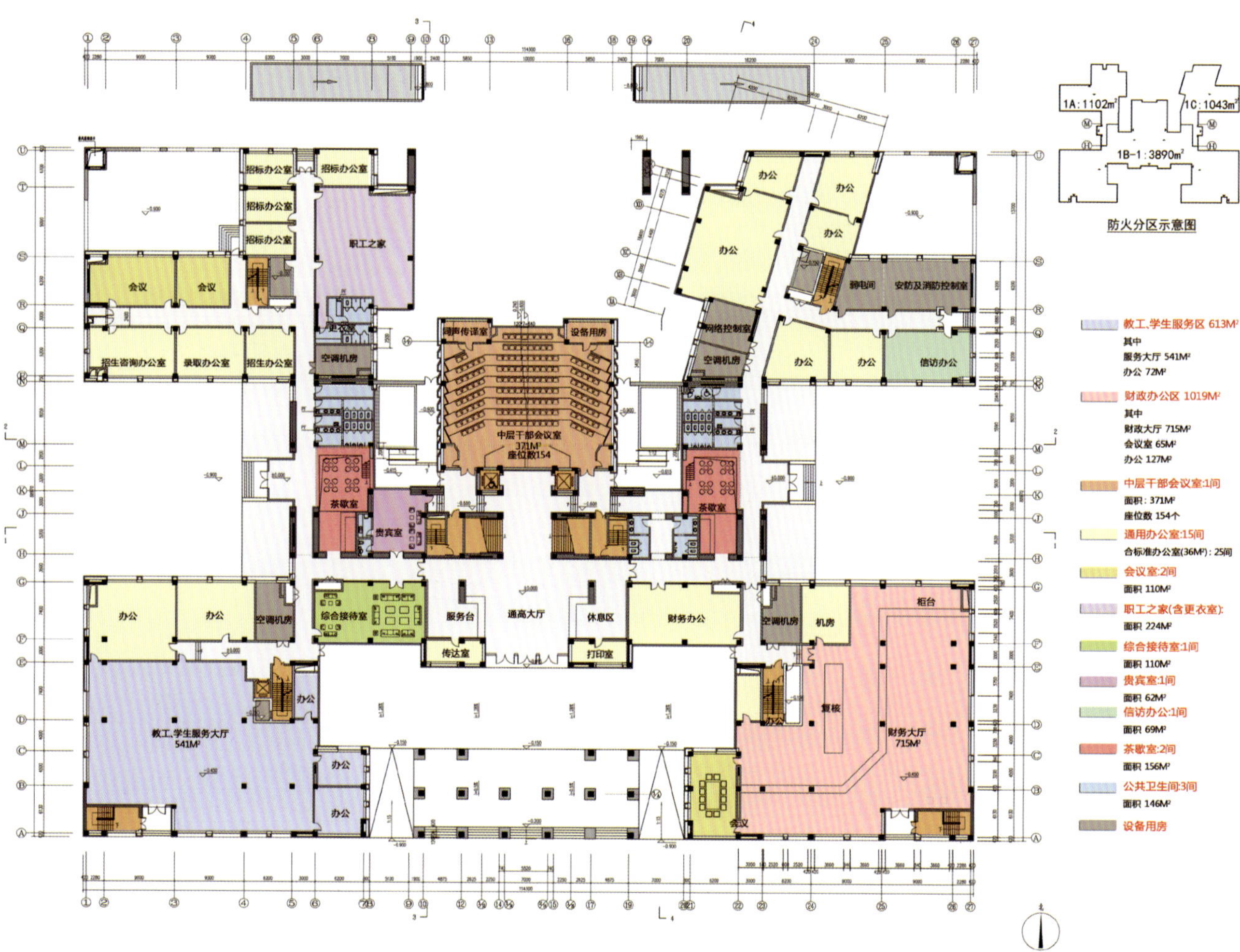

1895

Complex Gymnasium

综合体育馆

设计者:李兴钢、张音玄、闫昱、梁旭、易灵洁、唐勇、任庆英、张付奎、李森、赵昕、李建业、王微微、林佳

Designers: Li Xinggang, Zhang Yinxuan, Yan Yu, Liang Xu, Yi Lingjie, Tang Yong, Ren Qingying, Zhang Fukui, Li Sen, Zhao Xin, Li Jianye, Wang Weiwei, Lin Jia

综合体育馆位于校前区北侧，主要功能为满足日常体育教学科研及师生体育锻炼的需求，包括各种室内运动场地和教学、科研及配套设施用房以及室外田径场、各类球场、集中器械场地及极限运动场所。建筑主体包含室内体育活动中心和游泳馆两大部分，以一条跨街的大型缓拱形廊桥将两者的公共空间串连为一个整体，并形成一个环抱的入口广场，沟通建筑东西和南北。沿西立面首层展开的檐廊空间使室内运动场地向校园空间打开，成为良好的交往互动空间。建筑主体东侧设置若干室外运动场地，与相邻城市水系景观带自然过渡，并在主体北侧设置集中器械场、极限运动区等室外活动场地，被围合于建筑主体和北侧的游廊式建筑（含小卖服务及器械用房）之间。极限运动区通过不规则铺展的室外台阶看台，可以一直延伸到带有波浪形屋面（其下是室内体育活动中心的公共大厅）的建筑屋顶，如此成为一个室内与室外、地面与屋面连为一体的“全运动综合体”。

The Complex Gymnasium is located in the north side of campus front area, mainly to meet the demands for daily physical teaching and scientific research and physical exercises of teachers and students, including various indoor sports fields, rooms for teaching, scientific research, and supporting facilities, outdoor ground track field, various ball parks, instrument places, and extreme sports places. Major structure of the building includes indoor sports center and swimming pool, connecting two public spaces into an integral whole, to form a surrounding entrance square and to link the four directions of the building. Unfolded eaves gallery space makes indoor sport field open to campus space, to become favorable interaction space. Some outdoor sports fields are set in the east side of building structure, naturally transiting to city water-landscape belt nearby. Such outdoor playgrounds as concentrated instrument field and extreme sports area are set in the north side of the main body, enclosed between main building and arcade architecture (including snack services and instrument rooms) in the north. Extreme sports area can be extended to wave roof (public hall of indoor sports center below) through outdoor steps of irregular spreading. Therefore, it is a “full-motion complex” combining indoor and outdoor, as well as ground and roof as a whole.

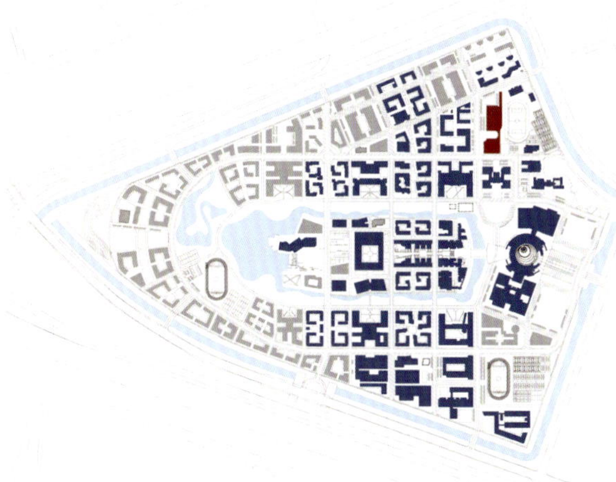

区位图

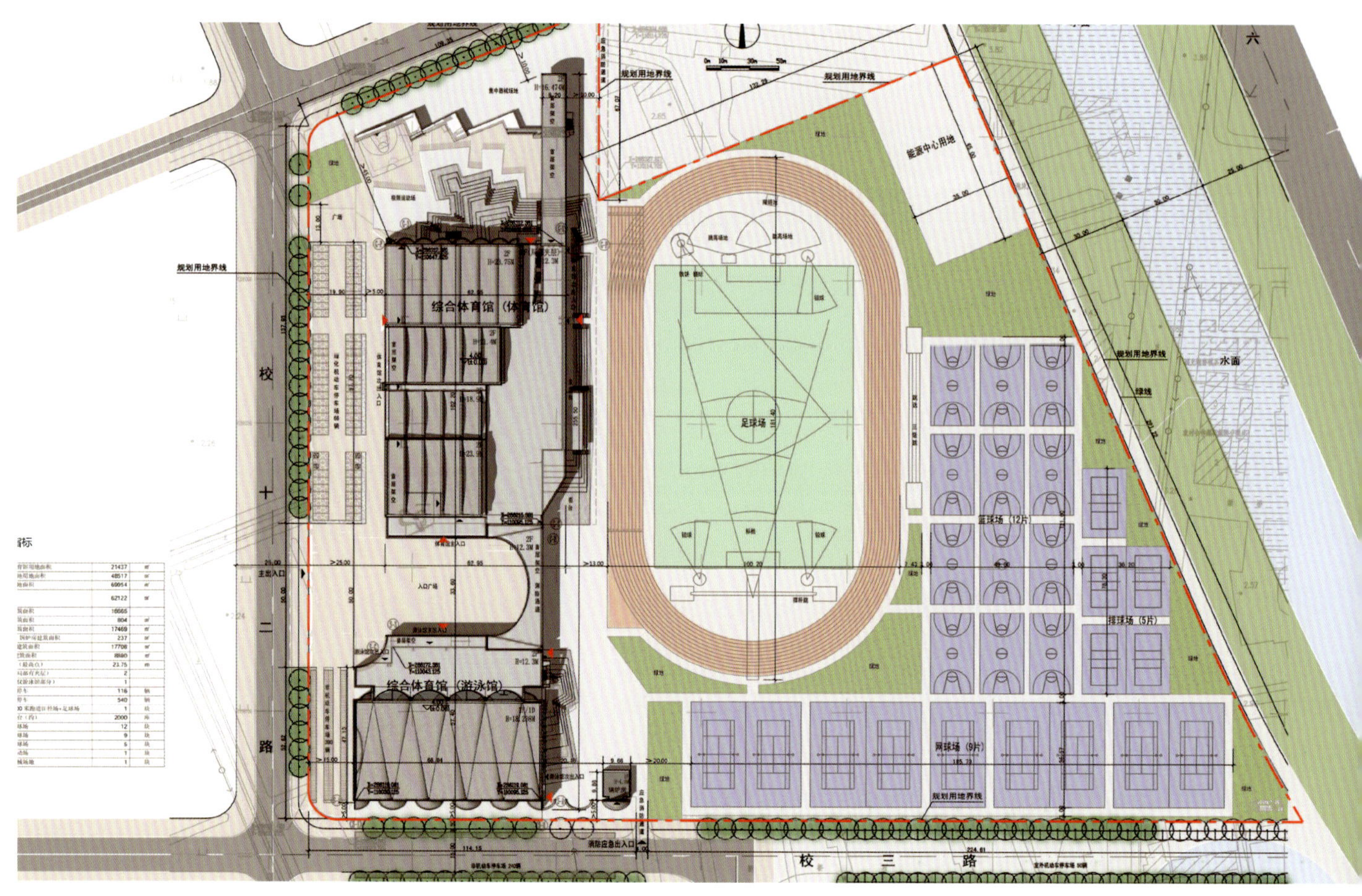

各类室内运动场地——排球场、网球场、篮球场、羽毛球场、径赛训练馆（室内跑道）、乒乓球馆、舞蹈馆、体操馆、健身馆、跆拳道馆、游泳馆等——依其对平面尺寸、净空高度及使用方式（专用或兼用）的不同要求，紧凑排列，并以线性公共空间（公共大厅、缓拱廊桥和游泳馆门厅）叠加、串联为一个整体，不仅增强了整个室内空间的开放性和运动氛围，而且天然造就了错落多样的建筑檐口高度，以及高效而舒展的平面布局。混凝土雨水沟槽沿着错落的建筑轮廓上下水平垂直明露设置，既可以看到雨落组织的导向，又成为独特的建筑压顶和收边。

Various indoor sports fields—Volleyball Court, Tennis Court, Basketball Court, Badminton Court, Track Training Center (indoor track), Table Tennis Hall, Dance Hall, Gym Hall, Gym, Taekwondo Gym, and Swimming Pool —are arranged compactly as their different requirements for plan size, head room, and usage mode (dedicated or dual-purpose), which are connected in an integrity as linear public spaces (Public Hall, Slow Arch Gallery Bridge, and Swimming Pool Hall). It not only increases openness and sports atmosphere of the whole indoor space but also creates diversified building eaves height and efficient and stretched plane layout. Concrete rainwater grooves are set vertically along building outline, through which we can see direction of rain falling organization.

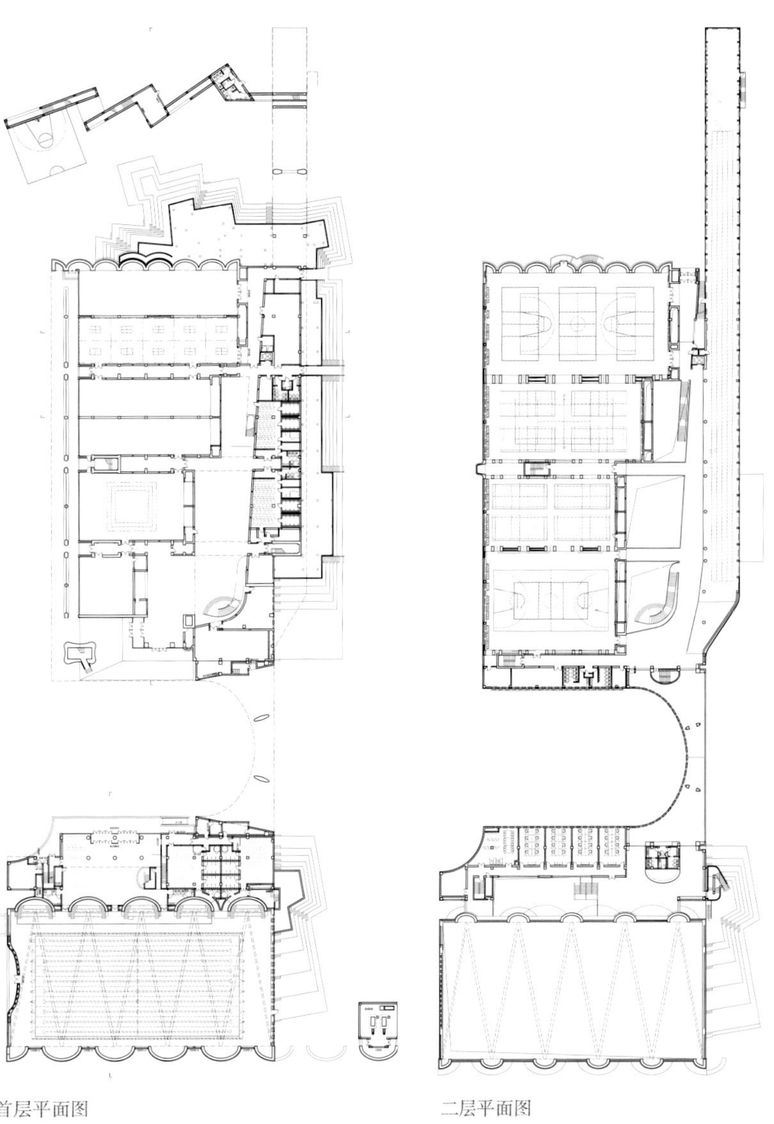

首层平面图　　二层平面图

室内体育中心的公共大厅屋面采用了波浪形渐变的直纹曲面形屋面（空心密肋屋盖结构），其东侧长达140米的室内跑道，不仅为大厅带来凸显屋面形状的自然光线和向远处延伸的外部景观，而且那些奔跑于架高跑道上的人，也成为可由室内外空间中欣赏的独特风景，彰扬建筑的运动主题。办公科研、淋浴更衣等辅助性空间以错层的方式布置在跑道上下，并在其外侧设面向室外田径运动场的室外看台及其主席台。大型廊桥的地面沿着平缓拱形的结构逐渐延伸，廊道西侧是沿弧线外墙规则排列的竖向窄条窗，朝向校园中心方向的入口广场；廊道东侧是随着地面起伏而延展的缓拱形横向长窗，朝向室外运动场及更远处的城市水系景观，这里也可以成为一个弹性、多功能的公共活动空间。游泳馆的入口公共空间是一个紧凑的中庭式空间，在上方靠近锥形薄壁柱体和顶部屋盖处，开出摆线形的天窗，照亮中庭和其中的楼梯。办公科研、淋浴更衣等辅助性空间临近馆池运动空间，并围绕中庭布置。

Public hall roof of indoor sports center adopts wavy gradient ruled surface roof (hollow multi-rib roof structure). The indoor track with 140m in length in the east brings natural light highlights roof shape and extended external landscape. Furthermore, people running on overhead runway become unique landscape appreciated interiorly and exteriorly. Such auxiliary spaces as office, scientific research, showering, and cloth changing are arranged around the runway in the way of staggered floor. Ground of large-scale gallery bridge extends gradually along gent and archy structure. Vertical fillet windows arranged regularly along arc exterior walls are in the west of gallery, towards entrance square of campus center; slow-arch long windows extending along the ground are in the east of gallery, towards outdoor sports field and farther city water system landscape, which can be an elastic and multi-functional public activity space. Entrance public space of the swimming pool is a compact atrium space, with a linear skylight close to taper thin-wall cylinder, lighting up the atrium and stairs. Such auxiliary spaces as office, scientific research, showering, and cloth changing are close to the swimming pool and embrace atrium.

运动场地空间的屋顶和外墙，使用了一系列直纹曲面、筒拱及锥形曲面的钢筋混凝土结构，带来大跨度空间和高侧窗采光，在内明露木模混凝土筑造肌理，在外形成沉静而多变的建筑轮廓。设计尝试强调在几何逻辑控制下对建筑基本单元形式和结构进行探寻，重复运用和组合这些单元结构，以生成特定功能、光线及氛围的建筑空间，并与学生的日常活动和外部的校园景观产生互动。

As for roof and outer wall of sport fields, a series of ruled surface, barrel vault, and taper cambered reinforced concrete structure are used, to bring large-span space and high side window lighting, with wood former concrete building texture inside and quiet and diversified building outline outside. Designers emphasize on exploring buildings' basic unit form and structure under control of geometrical logic to apply and combine such unit structures repeatedly, so as to generate building spaces with specific functions, rays, and atmosphere and to interact with students' daily activities and exterior campus landscape.

建筑外部材料主要采用清水混凝土饰面结合具有天津大学老校区建筑特色的深棕红色页岩砖拼贴饰面；室内各运动空间除露明本色混凝土肌理（墙柱和屋顶）及白色涂料（墙面和吊顶）的部位外，还采用了具有吸音功能的本色木丝板材墙面和本色欧松板材固定座椅，以增加空间的温暖感和舒适性。

External materials of buildings are mainly fair-faced concrete casing and brownish red shale bricks with building features of old campus of Tianjin University; besides parts using concrete texture (wall column and roof) and white paint (wall space and suspended ceiling), indoor motion spaces use natural wood-wool panel wall space and natural panel fixed seat with sound absorption functions, to increase spaces' sense of warmth and comfort.

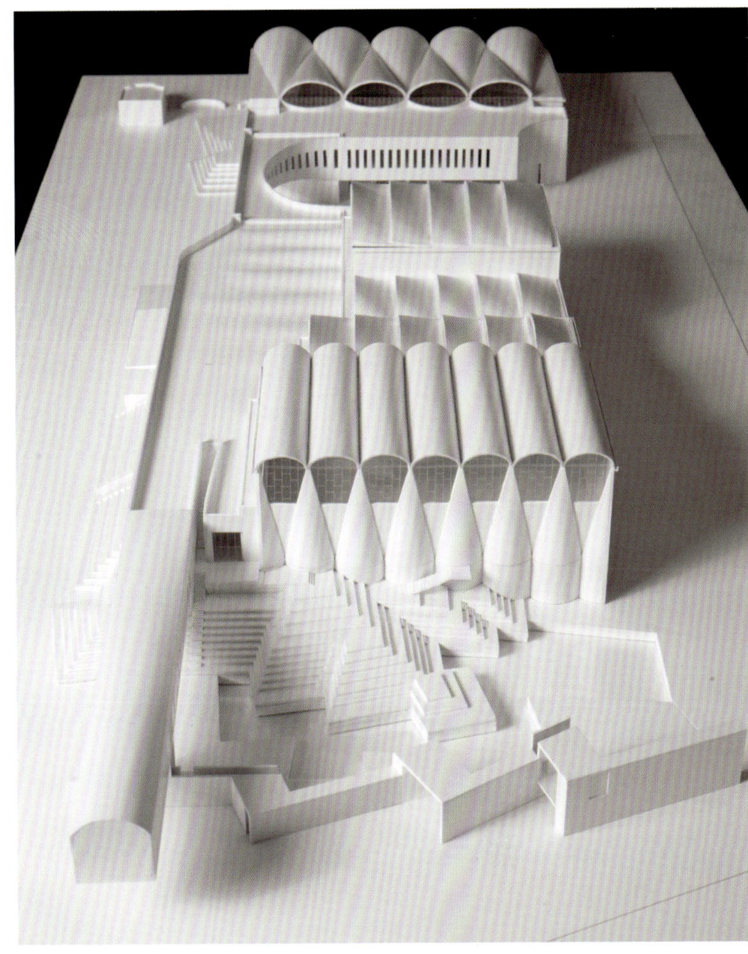

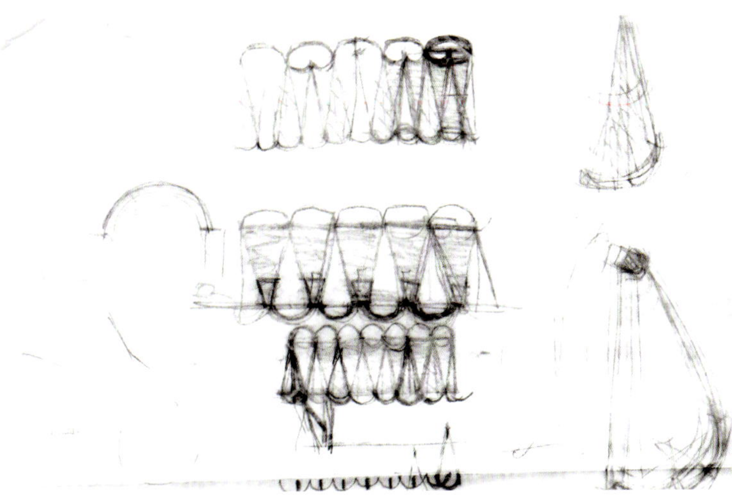

摄影：李兴钢

摄影：李兴钢

摄影：李兴钢

教学建筑

Teaching Building

Teaching Group of Water and Civil Engineering (38、39#)

水土建教学组团（38和39楼）

设计者：王兴田、杜富存、陈超、夏普、唐志华

Designers: Wang Xingtian, Du Fucun, Chen Chao, Xia Pu, Tang Zhihua

知行合一

颠覆既往大学校园将教学区、生活区、运动区明确分区的功能规划模式，以学院为单位将教学楼和学生生活区融合成基本单元体，有机生长的各单元体构成大校园。在每个单元体的教学楼和生活区之间导入属性暧昧的混沌空间，实现空间的有机过渡，完成行为的自然转换。建筑围合、半围合的广场、庭园为师生提供学习、生活等行为交流及活动的场所，并通过多层次交流环境的潜移默化，营造学生学习、生活、交往等社会活动为一体的寓教于乐的校园空间。

The unity of knowledge and action

Overturning the functional planning pattern of dividing the campus into teaching areas, living areas, and sports areas clearly in the past, the new campus of Tianjin University combines teaching buildings and students' living groups into basic units with the unit of college and the whole new campus is formed by organic units. Leading ambiguous chaos space into teaching buildings and living groups of each unit, to realize organic transition of space and to complete natural transformation of actions. Enclosed and semi-enclosed squares and gardens provide places for communication and activities of learning and daily life behaviors, to create an edutainment campus space combining students' learning, life, and association through unconscious influence of multi-level communication environment.

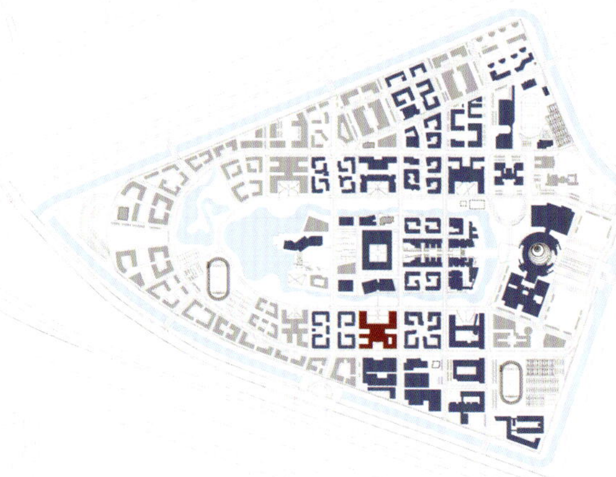

区位图

自然、开放空间

经历半个多世纪形成的老校区校园是留在校友脑海中抹不去的印象，试图营造那亲切、熟悉的场所空间，以适应北方寒冷地区的气候特征。整合各种类型的实验室，将重荷载，要求搬运出入便利的土木、环境实验室布置在一、二层，其上屋顶构成一个设置庭院、绿化的人工底盘。三层以上南北布局布置教学及教研室，建筑之间留出足够间距形成空中庭院，在充分满足自然通风、日照的同时，为师生提供一个亲近阳光、雨露的室外交流活动场所。

Nature, open space

The old campus formed for more than half a century is impressive to alumni. The design tries to create a cordial and familiar space to adapt to climatic characteristics in cold region of the north. Integrating labs of all types and arranging heavy load laboratories, civil engineering laboratories which are convenient for transportation, and environmental laboratories on 1/F and 2/F, a manual chassis with courtyard and greening on the roof is formed. Teaching and research offices are distributed above 3/F. Enough space is left between buildings to form a garden in the air, so as to offer a outdoor exchange activity place which is close to sunlight and raindrop.

新与旧

新校区教学楼将延续使用现存建筑给人深刻印象的“过火砖”为基本材料，局部植入素混凝土，以“土木”的表现力塑造一个稳重、简约、具有传承和记忆的建筑，底层架空的柱廊则创造出丰富的混沌空间和富有趣味的光影变化，让师生感受到时光的渐逝。

New and old

Teaching buildings of the new campus will continue to use impressive “burrs” as basic materials, implanting plain concrete partially, to shape a steady, contracted, inherited, and memorial building with the expressive force of “civil engineering”, and to create abundant chaos space and interesting shadow changes by overhead colonnades, so that teachers and students can feel to elapse of time.

室内外空间交融

通过中间共享中庭，连接南北两个半围合庭院。经过南广场、南门厅，一个舒缓的大台阶将人流引向建筑的主要使用层面——三层，两侧强调竖线肌理的墙面上布置了学院的历代教育家像，成为一个富有教育意义的空间。在此可重温天大双甲子历史和著名学科教育家及他们的研究成就，瞻仰先贤睿智，激励学子们实事求是、求真务实。

Blend of indoor and outdoor spaces

Two semi-enclosed courtyards are named in the north and south through the sharing courtyard in the middle. People are led to the main using floor(3F) of building through south plaza and south hall. Portraits of the educators across the generations are arranged on wall spaces of vertical-bar texture on both sides, to form a space with educational significance. Hereon, you can go over the history of 120 years and educators and their research achievements, to stimulate students to be practical and realistic through paying a visit to these wise men.

43

Practice Workshop of Water and Civil Engineering (40-43#)

水土建实习车间（40~43 楼）

设计者:曲晓舟、王文亮、张键、刘瑛

Designers: Qu Xiaozhou, Wang Wenliang, Zhang Jian, Liu Ying

水土建实习车间用地位于新校区南端，面向护校河和校外八纬路，属于新校区南侧教学区边缘区域。基地被南北方向校十路分为东西两个地块，西侧地块布置有水利工程实习车间、海洋与船舶工程实习车间、深水结构工程实习车间。东侧地块布置有港口与海岸工程实习车间、土木工程实习车间和设备用房。

设计着力处理建筑与其他区域便捷的联系问题以及自身内部交通的便捷问题，同时注重交通通达性，四周均设有入口，方便使用人群以及实验车辆到达。在用地内部，设计顺应实验需求设计了多样形态的庭院空间，建筑与地形结合紧密，使不同功能的实验室均获得较好的通风与采光。

各实习车间基本为单层建筑，空间组织构成以各实习车间主要实验区为中心作为主空间，沿各自周边布置对高度要求较低的各种实验辅助用房。主要实习区都与该实习车间室外缓冲场地有便捷的联系，方便实际使用中室内室外的功能联系。

建筑造型充分考虑与周边建筑形成协调一致的关系，对校内，考虑校园总体效果，与相邻教学建筑在风格和尺度上相协调；对校外，利用大尺度柱廊形成的规整的韵律感，弥合沿八纬路一侧实习建筑大小不一的建筑体量，既符合新校区规划总体建筑风格，又有所创新，整中有变，同中存异，形成舒展大方、典雅庄重的整体建筑形象。

The Practice Workshop of Water and Civil Engineering is located in the south end of the new campus, facing School Nursing River and Bawei Road, namely marginal area of teaching area in the south side of the new campus. The site is divided into two blocks by the Tenth Campus Road from south to north, with Hydraulic Engineering Practice Workshop, Shipbuilding and Offshore Engineering Practice Workshop, and Deep-water Structural Engineering Practice Workshop in the west, while with Port and Coastal Engineering Practice Workshop, Civil Engineering Practice Workshop, and Equipment Room in the east.

Designers focus on convenient connection between buildings and other areas, convenient and fast transportation, and accessibility of transportation. Furthermore, there are entrances in four directions, for the convenience of arrival of users and experiment vehicles. Interiorly, designers design diversified courtyard spaces and building and terrain integrate closely, so that labs of different functions can gain favorable ventilation and lighting.

Basically, all practice workshops are single-storey buildings. Main experimental areas of practice workshops are the center, with various labs around. Main practice areas have convenient connections to buffering areas outside practice workshops, for the convenience of indoor and outdoor functional connection.

As for architectural modeling, it is necessary to form compatible relationship with surrounding buildings. On campus, designers consider overall effects of campus, making it harmonious with adjacent teaching buildings in style and size; off campus, designers consider building mass formed by ordered rhythmical image and different practice buildings in size, namely meeting overall architectural style of the new campus and having innovations. Seeking common points while reserving differences, can form comfortable, elegant, and solemn monolithic architecture image.

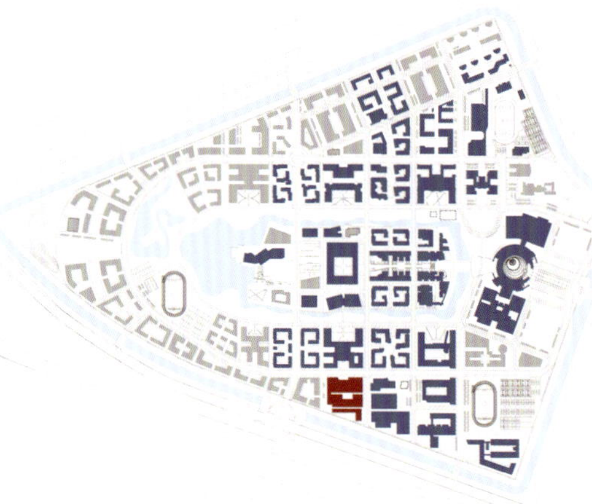

区位图

红线
1F 水利工程实习车间
海洋与船舶工程实习车间
1F 深水结构工程实习车间
工艺水池(地下)
港口与海岸工程实习车间河流动力实习区
港口与海岸工程实习车间
土木工程实习车间
护
校
河

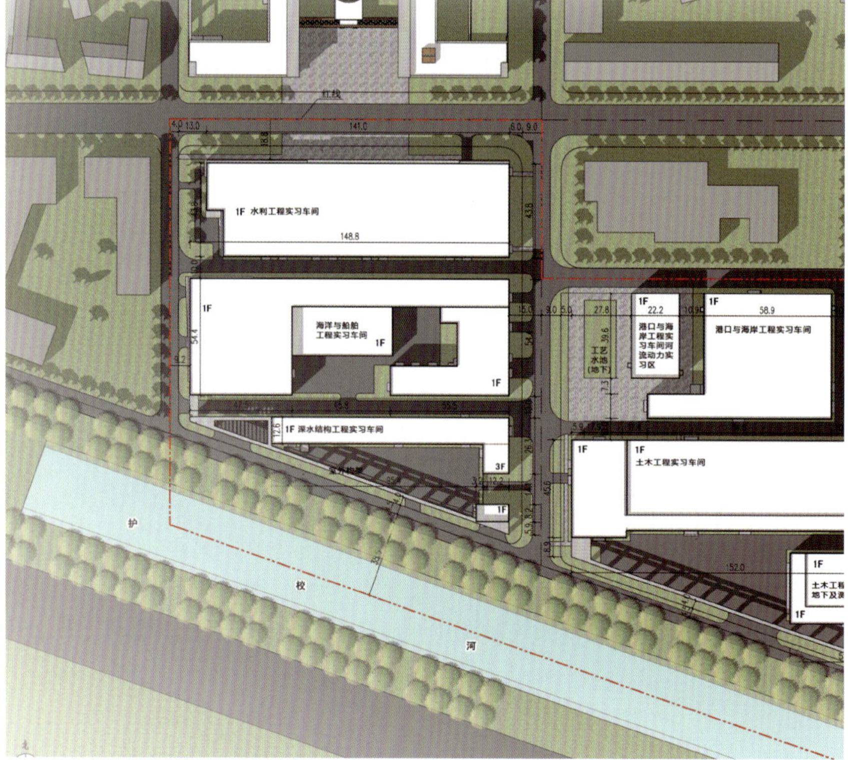

总平面图

Teaching Group of Chemical Engineering and Material (50-54#)

化工材料教学组团（50~54 楼）

设计者:张繁维、张大昕、柏新予、王光男

Designers: Zhang Fanwei, Zhang Daxin, Bo Xinyu, Wang Guangnan

化工材料教学组团根据区域分为化工南区和化工北区（理学院、材料学院两部分）。平面功能组成上，化工南区包括行政办公、专业教室和部分学院实验室与研究中心；化工北区则包括材料学院新材料实验楼、理学院实验中心和部分国家重点实验室以及研究中心。化工学院南区采用对称式整体平面构成，围合成多个空间舒展的内庭院和半开放式庭院。主入口正对湖心岛，立面端庄大方，极具标志性，整体立面造型较为传统，对天津大学老校区的建筑有一定的传承，风格稳健大气。

化工学院北区则处理得相当简练，几个不同体块穿插、围合，形成不同的外庭院空间，为各学院学生提供了相互学习和交流的机会。结合实验室的平面模数，立面设计以竖直线条作为母题贯穿始终，简洁现代。南北区两种风格形成鲜明的对比，传统与流行并重，具有较强的认知性，成为化工材料教学组团独有的形象设计亮点。建筑墙体材料为砖红色面砖，与新校区整体形象与环境相契合。

Regionally, Teaching Group of Chemical Engineering and Material is divided into Southern Chemical Engineering Region and Northern Chemical Engineering Region. In plane functional composition, Southern Chemical Engineering Region includes administrative offices, classrooms, and labs and research centers; Northern Chemical Engineering Region includes New Material Laboratory Building of Material School, Experiment Center of School of Science, and some national key laboratories and research centers. Southern Chemical Engineering Region adopts symmetric overall plane to enclose interior courtyard and semi-enclosed courtyards. The main entrance faces Mid-lake Island directly, whose facade is dignified, magnanimous, symbolic, and traditional, which inherits buildings of old campus of the Tianjin University to some extent.

However, Northern Chemical Engineering Region is very concise, where several different blocks intersperse and enclose to form different exterior courtyard spaces, to provide chances for mutual learning and exchange of students. With the combination of plate modules of labs, elevation design regards vertical lines as theme, which is concise and modern. Two styles of southern and northern regions are in stark contrast, paying equal attention to tradition and popularity. With strong cognition, it becomes particular image design bright of Chemical Engineering and Material Teaching Group. Building wall materials are brick-red face bricks, which agrees with the overall image and environment of the new campus.

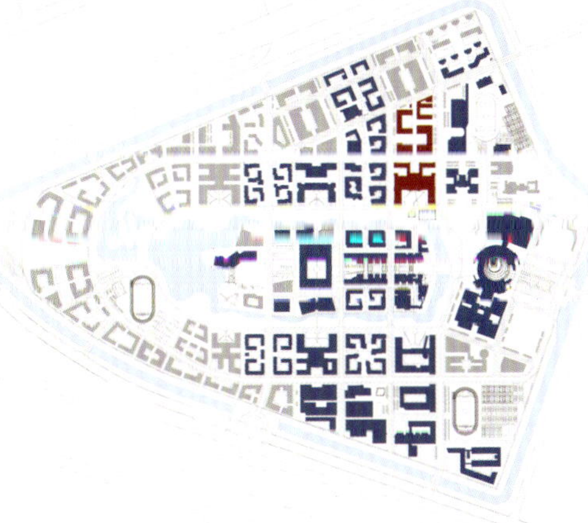

区位图

52

Machinery Teaching Group (34-37#)

机械教学组团（34~37楼）

设计者:顾志宏、张大昕、柏新予、王建午

Designers: Gu Zhihong, Zhang Daxin, Bai Xinyu, Wang Jianwu

在整个天津大学新校区里，由于机械学科自身的特点，必然对机械教学组团的建筑设计提出独特的功能要求，机械组团可以说是天津大学新校区中教育建筑和工业建筑相互结合的典型代表。

机械教学组团位于整个校园的“东南角”，结合总体校园规划，机械组团分为4个组成部分：由北至南为机械学院综合楼、力学大楼、实践教学中心和热动力大楼。兼具办公教学主楼性质的综合楼采取优雅的均衡建筑构图，面向校园内的主要道路，而其他各类实验厂房位于学院组团的南侧，尽量减少对校园内部的干扰。4个组成部分既保持相对独立，又在设计中引入一个“绳结”的概念，把4个地块中用内庭院组织的建筑空间串连起来，形成了一个和谐的整体建筑群。

外墙材料以面砖为主，局部点缀金属构件，形成素雅的建筑立面，使这组建筑在融入整个天津大学新校区校园环境的同时，含蓄地表达出了机械学科的特点。

In the new campus of Tianjin University, we are certain to raise unique functional requirements for the architectural design of Machinery Teaching Group because of the characteristics of machinery. People can say that it is a typical example for the combination of educational building and industrial building in the new campus of Tianjin University.

Machinery Teaching Group is located in the “southwest corner” of the whole campus. With the combination of overall campus planning, the machinery group is divided into four constituent parts, namely Complex Building of Mechanics Institute, Mechanics Building, Practical Teaching Center, and Thermo-motive Building from north to south. The Complex Building, having the nature of office and teaching building, adopts elegant balanced architectural composition and face main roads in the campus. However, lab factories of other types are located in the south of college group, to reduce disturbances to inner campus. Four constituent parts can not only keep relatively independent but also bring into the concept of “clinch” in design. Such four plots are connected with the use of building space organized by interior courts, to form a harmonious overall building group.

Exterior wall materials are mainly face bricks, with mental components partially, to form plain building elevation, so that this group of building can implicitly express the features of mechanical subject when blending into the whole new campus environment of Tianjin University.

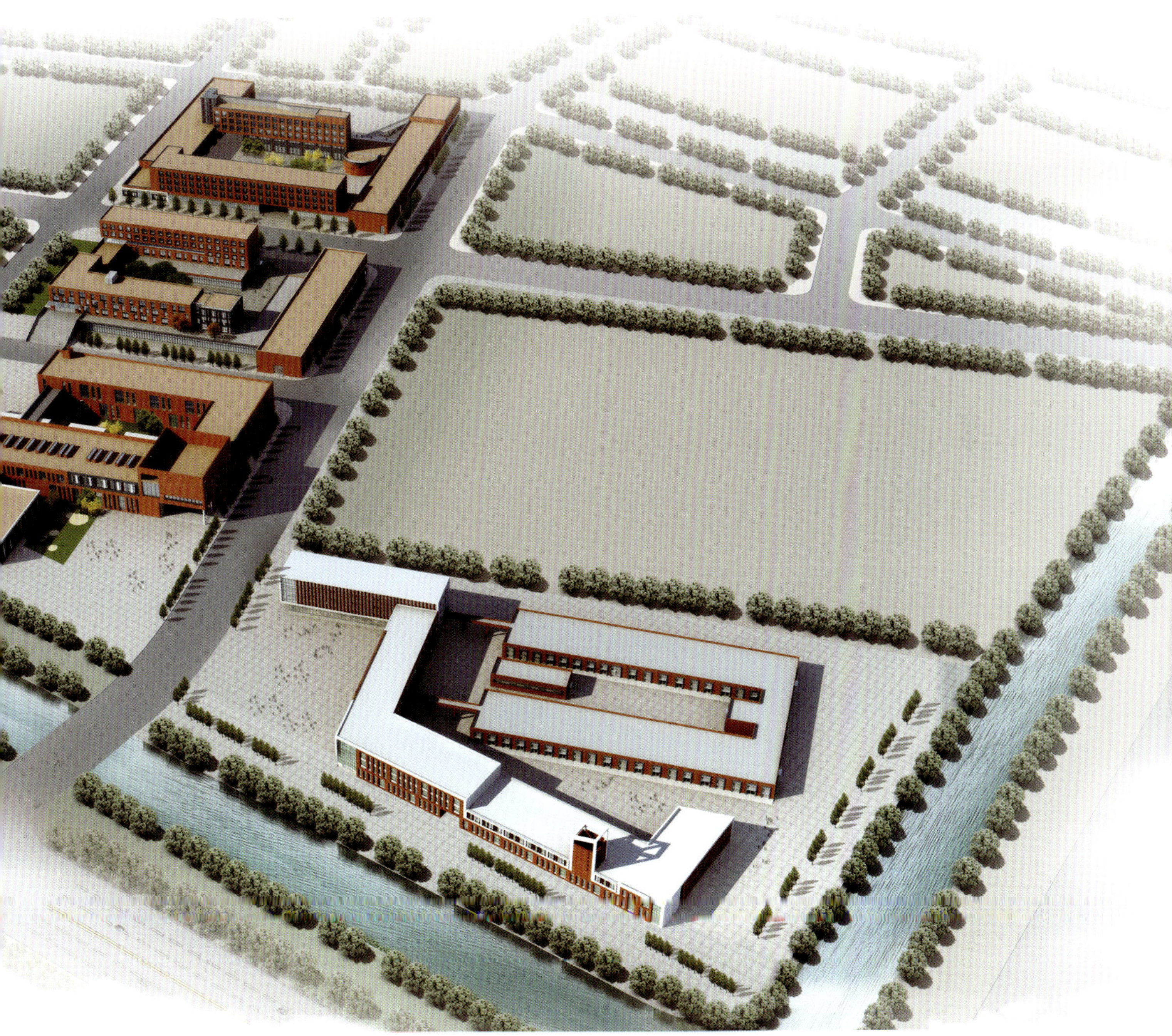

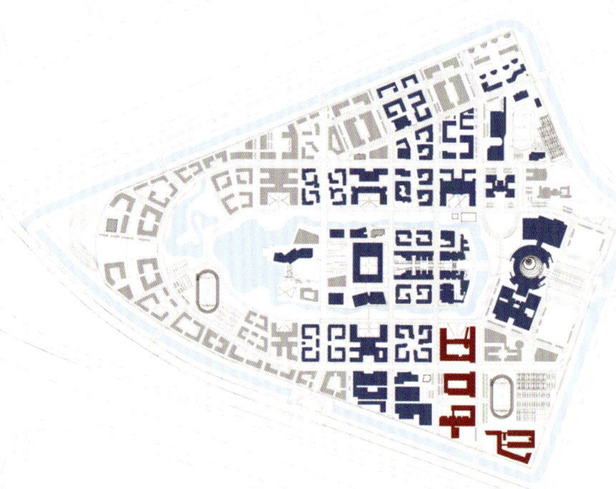

区位图

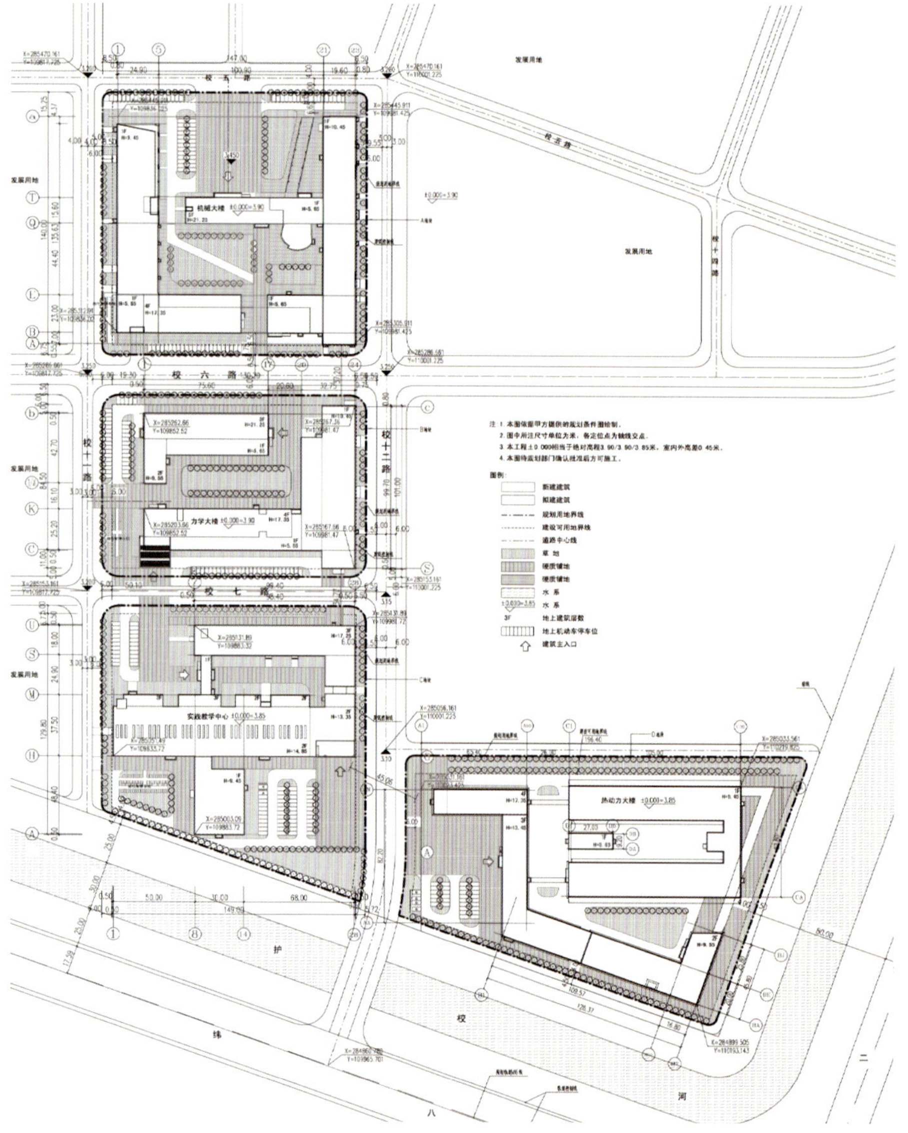

总平面图

Teaching Group of Computer and Software (55#)

计算机软件教学组团（55楼）

设计者：卞洪滨、张波、于泳、镡新、冯卫星、张在方

Designers: Bian Hongbin, Zhang Bo, Yu Yong, Chan Xin, Feng Weixing, Zhang Zaifang

计算机学院和软件学院教学楼位于公共教学核心区北侧，与图书馆隔河相望，两个学院建筑面积合计为21000㎡，其北侧为预留二期用地。

为体现两个学院的平等、共生，建筑总体布局遵循校园城市设计导则的要求，左右对称呈U字形布局，围合出宽敞、沉静的南部院落。建筑主体5层，两侧副楼3层高。建筑中轴处布置入口大厅、休息厅、会议室等公共空间，以强化两个学院的共享、共融。计算机和软件学院分置两侧，各有独立的展示、交流空间。

结合分体空调室外机的安放位置，建筑外部肌理利用横竖两种窗洞组合，来隐喻二进制的0、1这两个基本的算符，以此来体现现代的计算机和软件技术所采用的二进制的学科特点。

Teaching buildings of School of Computer Science and Technology and School of Computer Software are located in the north core area of public school building, facing the library from the other side of the river. Building area of the two schools is 21,000 ㎡, whose north side is the reserved land of phase II.

In order to reflect equality and mutualism of two schools, the overall layout of the building abides by the requirements of campus urban design guidelines, being distributed in "U" shape and enclosing roomy and quiet south courtyard. Major structure of the building has five floors, while annex building has three floors. Building axis place is arranged with entrance hall, lobby, and assembly room, so as to intensify sharing and co-fusion of two schools. The two schools are in each side, with independent exhibition and exchange space.

With the combination of placing position of air condensing units, exterior texture of the building metaphors 0 and 1 of binary system, to reflect subject characteristics of binary system taken by modern computer and software technology.

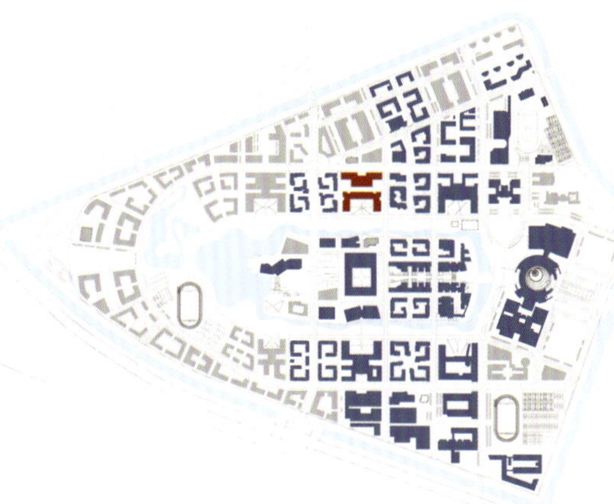

区位图

计算机学院

生活建筑

Living Building

学生生活组团主要包括中区、北区、南区、东区、西区、硕士生公寓组团和博士生公寓组团。根据建筑围合排序，共计分为24斋。学生生活组团参考中国传统文化元素命名，在传统典籍《大学》中描述了君子成长成才的过程：格物、致知、诚意、正心、修身、齐家、治国、平天下，将24斋按组团命名为格园、知园、诚园、正园、修园、齐园、治园和平园。

新校区共设有8个食堂。食堂以寓意美好的植物为命名元素，其中学三和学五食堂附近为海棠树和桃花树，故命名为“棠园”和“桃园”，其余4个学生食堂以中国传统文化中寓意高洁的梅兰竹菊“四君子”为名，分别为学一（梅园）、学二（兰园）、学四（竹园）和学六（菊园）。留学生食堂和教师食堂则分别以“留园”（邻近留学生公寓）和“青园”（邻近青年教师公寓）命名。

Student living groups mainly include established central, north, south, east, west living group, master student living group and doctor student living group. There are 24 apartments in all according to building order. Names of student living groups were made mainly referring to Chinese traditional cultural elements. In The Great Learning, the process for gentlemen to grow is as follows: investigate and research things, learn knowledge, be sincere, be honest, cultivate moral character, govern family, manage state affairs, and unite the world, so the 24 apartments were named as Ge Garden, Zhi Garden, Cheng Garden, Zheng Garden, Xiu Garden, Qi Garden, Zhi Garden, and Ping Garden.

There are eight canteens in new campus. Canteens are named with nice plants' names. Furthermore, there are cherry-apple trees and peach blossoms beside the 3rd and 5th students' Canteen, so they are called as "Cherry-apple Garden Canteen" and "Peach Garden Canteen". The other four canteens are named with "four gentlemen" in Chinese traditional culture. They are the 1st (plum blossoms), 2nd (orchid), 4th (bamboo), 6th (chrysanthemum) Canteen. Overseas students' canteen and teachers' canteen are named as "Liu Garden Canteen" (adjacent to Overseas Students' Apartment) and "Youth Garden Canteen" (adjacent to Young Teachers' Apartment).

East Living Group

东区生活组团

设计者:张大昕、王江飞、王庆东

Designers: Zhang Daxin, Wang Jiangfei, Wang Qingdong

东区生活组团位于新校区东北角地块，分两期建设，其功能一是解决博士后人员及学校新引进人才周转租住宿舍，二是解决部分新入校辅导员及其他工作人员宿舍，三是配套教工食堂及校医院。在整体布局上，邻近校园主路的建筑为多层，其底层设计服务于整个区域的商铺、餐饮、物业等用房，并在邻近校园出入口的部分形成开敞的集散空间。后侧为塔式住宅，与多层宿舍及食堂形成相对围合的半私密空间。立面设计上，如何与新校区外部环境的协调对接成为设计的重点，故设计采用简约的古典设计风格，传统的坡屋顶形式也与居住建筑的性质相吻合。校园主路南侧的校医院建筑布局采用合院式，合理分配了建筑功能的总流线需求，通过回廊布置，形成了丰富多彩的内部空间。立面采用生态木与砖相结合的形式，表现建筑厚重内敛的性格及绿色生态构造精致的特点。

East living group is located in the northeast corner of the new campus, which has been built in two phases. Its functions are (1) to turn-around dormitories for post doctors and newly brought talents; (2) to provide dormitories for new instructors and other staffs; (3) to support teachers' canteen and school infirmary. In overall layout, buildings close to main campus roads are multi-layer, whose ground floor serves as stores, catering, and property of the whole area, forming an open gathering and distributing space closing to campus entrance. There are tower dwellings in the back, to form a semi-private space together with multi-layer dormitories and dinning hall. In elevation design, how to coordinate with external environment of the new campus is a key in design, so simple classical feature and traditional pitched roof are adopted. Hospital building in the south of the main road is in the style of courtyard, which reasonably distributes total flow line demands of building function. Colorful inner space is formed through layout of winding corridor. The elevation combines ecological wood and bricks to show dignified and restraining character and green ecology.

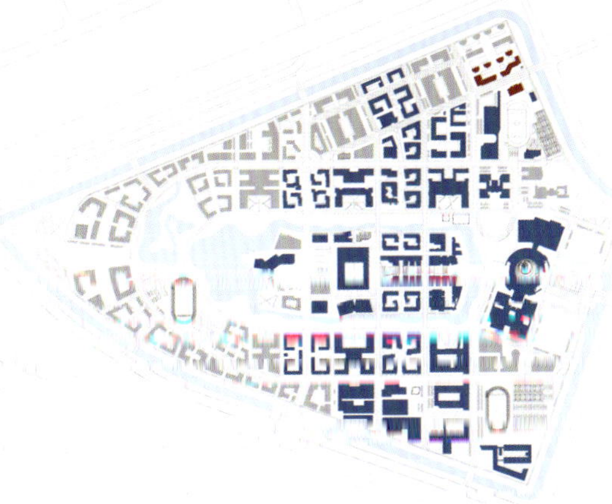

区位图

South Living Group

南区生活组团

设计者：姜维、刘越、郭鹏伟、抗莉君、杜春枝、卫东、单瑞增、位力强、李芊、柯加林、柴庆、迟珊

Designers: Jiang Wei, Liu Yue, Guo Pengwei, Kang Lijun, Du Chunzhi, Wei Dong, Shan Ruizeng, Wei Liqiang, Li Qian, Ke Jialin, Chai Qing, Chi Shan

宿舍和食堂是与学生日常生活最息息相关的功能组团，但往往又是整个校园建筑中最容易被忽视的部分，常会受到很大的限定和制约，如何在妥协与权衡中塑造"恰到好处"的高质量空间成为本设计的核心。

宿舍区由两幢本科公寓及两幢硕士公寓组成，遵循"一成二、二生四"的设计初衷，形成沿基地周边向心式的风车状总体布局。宿舍内部使用功能力求简约实用，采取方正的形态和紧凑的空间，争取最大的使用效率及经济性。活动室、自习室、咖啡厅等不同属性的公共功能被不同私密层级的景观元素组织起来，形成完整的群落聚合体，中心集中绿化广场作为聚合体的核心不断传达出整个场域的张力和多元性，为学生们丰富的课余活动提供多可能性的平台。

第四学生食堂位于宿舍区的南侧，主入口广场与宿舍中心集中绿化广场遥相呼应。内部就餐区与厨房区南北分置，合理的功能整合与流线的组织很大程度上削弱了瞬间人流量对就餐空间的压迫。门厅北侧的对景庭院及入口处的室外就餐平台均作为小尺度的空间传达着舒适恬淡的建筑姿态。

属于建筑师的设计也许完成了，但属于使用者的设计才刚刚开始。

Dormitory and canteen are closely bound up with students' daily life, which are easily ignored in the whole campus design and may be limited and restrained greatly. How to shape "to-the-point" high-quality space in compromise and balance is the core of the design.

Dormitory area is made up of two bachelor apartments and two master apartments, to form windmill entire layout. Internal using functions of dormitory should be simple and practical, adopting quadrate form and compact space to strive for the maximum service efficiency and economical efficiency. Public functions of different properties, such as activity rooms, study rooms, and coffee houses, are organized by landscape elements of different privacy levels, to form integrated colony. As the core of the polymer, the center green square conveys tension and diversity of the whole field, so as to provide many possible platforms for students' rich extracurricular activities.

The fourth student canteen is in the south side of dormitory area. Main entrance square and center green square echo each other at a distance. Interior dinning area and kitchen area are located in the north and south separately, and reasonable functional integration and streamlined organization can weaken oppression of moment visitors flow rate to diet space. Scenery courtyard in the north of entrance hall and outdoor dining platform at the entrance convey comfortable and tranquil architectural gesture.

Architect design may be finished, but user ' s design just starts.

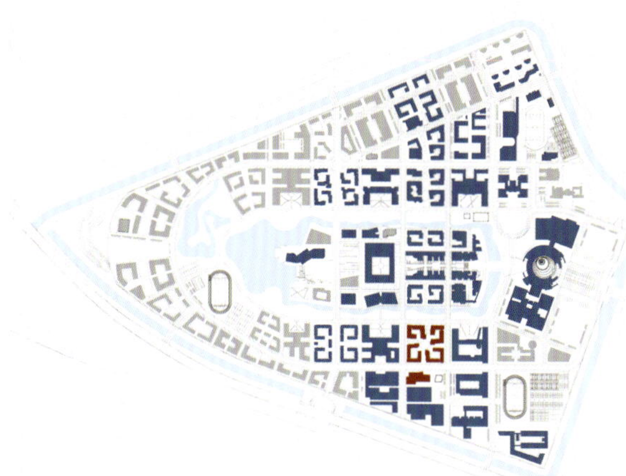

区位图

West Living Group
西区生活组团

设计者:王重、任军、石岩、陈然、肖向东、朱皓

Designers: Wang Zhong, Ren Jun, Shi yan, Chen Ran, Xiao Xiang dong, Zhu Hao

西区生活组团主要包括本科生公寓、留学生公寓和学生食堂。

延续校区的轴线肌理，在地块内设置了南北向的景观带。建筑沿景观带布置，并采用围合式，形成内庭院空间。留学生公寓位于地块北侧沿河，景观条件优越。本科生公寓分别位于主景观带两侧，形成不同开口方向的院落，统一且富有变化。食堂位于地块的西南侧，与景观带相邻，既便于人流疏散，又有较好的景观。设计中，区别于其他组团的食堂设计，尤其在二层设置了餐饮及活动露台，突出公共建筑的活泼形式，结合未来留学生及本科学生的使用，为丰富课余生活提供一个人性化的交往活动空间。景观设计延续校园景观轴，在组团之间形成了共享的绿化景观并与组团内庭院互动，创造优美的校园居住空间。西区生活组团与整体规划建筑风格相协调，外檐主材采用仿面砖涂料，立面形式简洁大气，突出宿舍建筑的特质，在整体校园中低调、静谧。

West living group mainly includes undergraduate apartments, overseas students' apartments, and student canteen.

Extending axis texture of the campus, landscape belt from south and north is set in the block. Buildings are set along the landscape belt and enclosure is used to form interior courtyard space. Overseas students' apartments are located in the north side of the block, with excellent landscape conditions. Undergraduate apartments are located in two sides of landscape belt, to form courtyards of different opening directions. The student canteen is located in the southwest of the block, bordering upon the landscape belt, which is convenient for crowd evacuating and has better landscape. Catering and activity terrace on the second floor are designed, to highlight lively form of public buildings, to enrich after-school life, and to provide a humanized interactive space. The main landscape belt interacts with courtyard, to create graceful campus living space. West living group coordinates with the overall planning architectural style. Main materials of exterior eaves are face-brick coating, and the elevation style is concise, to highlight characteristics of dormitory building, which is low-key and quiet.

North Living Group

北区生活组团

设计者：赖军、任思鸣、李林、王敬、谢琳、薛昆、岳艳刚、张凯、聂亚飞、文柳、刘路平

Designers: Lai Jun, Ren Siming, Li Lin, Wang Jing, Xie Lin, Xue Kun, Yue Yangang, Zhang Kai, Nie Yafei, Wen Liu, Liu Luping

传统宿舍采用行列式布局，不便于人与人之间的交往，在这样的场所中，学生课外活动变得单一，缺乏活力，很难打破以往三点一线的单调的生活方式。本设计以学生生活为中心，创造半开放式的院落空间。院落的第一层次为半开放的广场，利于人流的集散；院落的第二层次为相对私密的生活交往空间，让学生们在组团内部形成轻松愉悦的氛围。

Traditional dormitories adopt row layout, which is inconvenient of communication between people. In such place, students' extracurricular activities become boring and are lack of vitality, so that it is difficult to break through the unexciting life of "three points and one line" before. The design regards student life as the center, to create semi-open courtyard space. The first layer of courtyard is semi-open square, which is in favor of gathering and distributing people stream; the second layer of courtyard is relatively private life contact space, so that students can experience easy and funny atmosphere within the group.

Central Living Group

中区生活组团

设计者:王重、任军、石岩、陈然、肖向东、朱皓

Designers: Wang Zhong, Ren Jun, Shi Yan, Chen Ran, Xiao Xiangdong, Zhu Hao

中区生活组团主要功能包括5、6组团公寓、食堂和宿管中心。规划布局采用围合式，5、6组团公寓分别形成了两个内庭院空间，并在两组团相邻处设置了景观延伸至水面，整体设计统一且富有变化。组团围合的方式也更加强调了宿舍空间的归属感，祥和安静。食堂及宿管中心布置在地块的东侧，交通便捷。在建筑占地面积较大的情况下，在食堂用地的西南角设置了入口广场，在满足疏散功能的同时，营造出入口空间氛围。宿管中心与食堂围合布局，形成食堂后院，便于实际使用与隐蔽。

在景观设计上，组团内着重处理内庭院空间，并将景观与晾晒等使用空间相结合设计。在两公寓组团之间设计了共享庭院，丰富了室外庭院空间，创造出优美的校园空间。建筑风格与整体规划相协调。建筑形体简洁，在檐口、窗台等细部处理体现出精细的设计，外檐主要材质选用仿面砖涂料，体现出校园建筑的稳重与典雅。

Central living group includes the 5th and 6th group apartments, student canteen, and Dormitory Management Center. The layout is enclosed. The 5th and 6th group apartments form two interior courtyard spaces respectively and landscapes on the adjacent place of two groups are set, which extend to the water surface. The enclosed way emphasizes the sense of belonging of dormitory space, which is harmonious and quiet. Student canteen and Dormitory Management Center are in the east of the block, with convenient transportation. As the building area is large, entrance square is set in the southwest corner of student canteen, to meet the function of evacuation and to create space atmosphere of entrance and exit. Dormitory Management Center and student canteen are enclosed, to form backyard of student canteen, for the convenience of actual use and concealment.

In landscape design, it emphasizes to deal with interior courtyard space and combine landscape and airing. Sharing courtyard is designed between two apartments, which enriches outdoor courtyard space and creates beautiful campus space. Architectural style and overall planning coordinate with each other. Building shape is concise. Detailed design is embodied in cornices and windowsills. The main materials of exterior eaves are face-brick coating, to embody dignity and elegance of campus buildings.

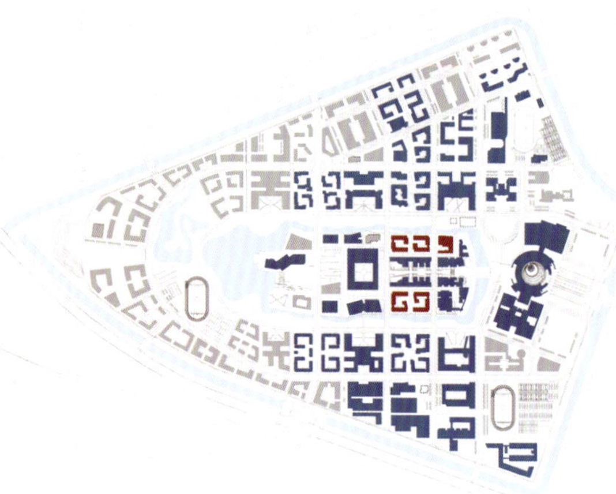

区位图

Living Group for Master Student

硕士生公寓组团

设计者：王戈、张镝鸣、王鹏、马笛、李洁苒、郭鹏伟、赵甜甜

Designers: Wang Ge, Zhang Diming, Wang Peng, Ma Di, Li Jieran, Guo Pengwei, Zhao Tiantian

形象：质朴与简洁

延续天津大学百年传承下来的建筑风格：质朴、简洁、大气，舒展。不倚重宿舍外在立面形式，而把注意力放在关注宿舍内部空间的舒适性和外部空间的整体性，以及由此带来的亲切感。

精神：交流与共享

宿舍不再简单是给学生休息的地方，在新的时代，宿舍将为学生创造更多的交往空间和交流场所——即“网络化”的生活状态。这里有内部活动室、公共自习室、超市、咖啡饮品店、室外露台……

愿景：学习型社区

沉静和活跃气氛并存的未来学府，要求新型宿舍空间里应有更多的公共属性。宿舍设计注重在给学生带来温暖和庇护的同时，创造了学习型社区的模式：简朴又充满活力，成为真正适合大学生活的地方。

Image: plain and concise

It continues architectural styles of Tianjin University inherited for one hundred years: plain, concise, grand, and stretched. It doesn” t rely on external facades form of dormitories, but pays attention to the comfort of dormitories’ inner space and integrality of outer space, as well as intimacy brought by this.

Spirit: communication and sharing

Dormitory is not only the place for students to have a rest, but also will create more contact space and exchange place for students in the new era, namely “networking” living conditions. There are interior activity rooms, public study rooms, supermarkets, coffee and drinks stores, and outdoor terraces, etc.

Vision: learning community

In future university with quiet and active atmosphere, new dormitory space shall have more public properties. Dormitory pays attention to the creation of the model of learning community when bringing warmness and shield for students: simple but lively, to become the places really suitable for master students.

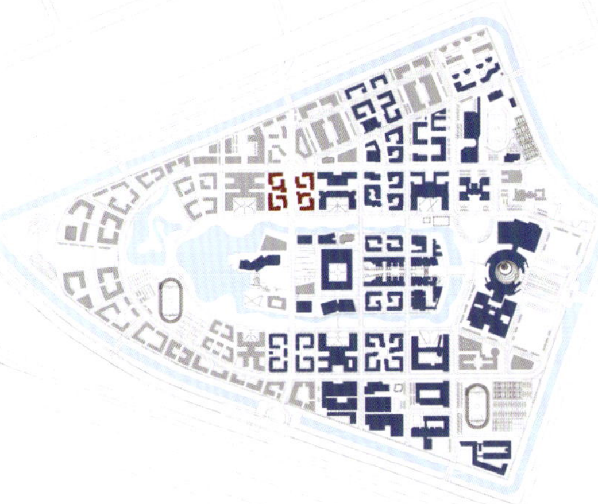

区位图

Living Group for Doctor Student

博士生公寓组团

设计者:张弛、闻锦程、白媚

Designers: Zhang Chi, Wen Jincheng, Bai Mei

博士生公寓组团紧临天津大学新校区南大门，东临水土建教学组团，隔河远眺北洋音乐厅，校际联络线从中穿越，位置十分重要。建筑规划为两个“8”字形的空间形态，主体分成4个组团，组团间以道路分成街区。每一个组团都采用内庭院、坡屋顶的传统建筑形式的布局。4个居住空间彼此开放又相对独立，总图排布如窗花一般，由不同庭院、建筑连廊有机镶嵌，雕琢间尽显张力。

根据现代大学生比较“宅”的生活特点，建筑设计体现了新时代大学生活特征，生活学习并重，最大限度地考虑多种公共交往场所，以方便学生交流。例如，每一公寓组团底层平面均设有公共大厅、休息室、商铺等。同时，每层都设有学生活动室、洗衣房、眺望厅等，方便学生社交活动。

平面功能方面，宿舍按不同班级划分成若干个居住单元，每12~15户学生公寓组成一个居住单元，每一单元通过连廊或过厅等公共区域彼此相互联系，既保证了单元的私密、统一，又方便了各个单元的联系，也利于校方实行班级管理。

建筑形态方面，立面统一采用坡屋面简约三段式设计，深灰色坡屋面、砖红色面砖、浅乳白色外墙涂料、玛瑙灰的铝合金门窗与空调格栅，形成极其绚丽、质朴、厚实的独特立面风格。建筑虚实对比适度，冷暖色彩搭配协调，整体性突出。建筑形态不仅赋予北洋建筑旧貌的独有气质，同时，新建筑的稳妥与谦逊，端庄与大气是对百年天大厚朴底蕴的尊重与升华。

Living Group for Doctor Student is next to south gate of the new campus of Tianjin University, close to Civil Engineering and Water Teaching Group to the east and overlooking Peiyang Music Hall, and its position is very important. The site planning is two 8-shaped forms. The main body is divided into four groups. Each group adopts the traditional layout of inner courtyard and slopping roof. Four living spaces are open and independent, set by different courtyards and building corridors.

In accordance with the living characteristics that modern university students are relatively "indoorsy", the design emphasizes on public places for students to communicate. For example, there are public halls, lounges, and stores in the ground floor of each apartment group. And at the same time, there are student activity rooms, laundry rooms, and overlooking halls on each floor, for the convenience of students' social activities.

As for floor plan, dormitories are divided into several residential units according to different classes and each group of 12-15 student apartments forms a residential unit. Units connect each other through corridors or galleries, which guarantees units' privacy, unity and convenience for communication and class management.

As for architectural form, the facades adopt concise three-stage sloping-roof design. The dark grey pitched roof, brick-red face brick, light milk white exterior wall coating, alloy door and window and air-conditioning grids of agate grey, together form gorgeous, plain, and thick unique elevation style. Buildings' virtual-real comparison is proper, cold and warm color is coordinate, and integrality is highlighted. Architectural form gives not only unique property of old Peiyang buildings but also reliable, modest, dignified, and generous property of the new buildings.

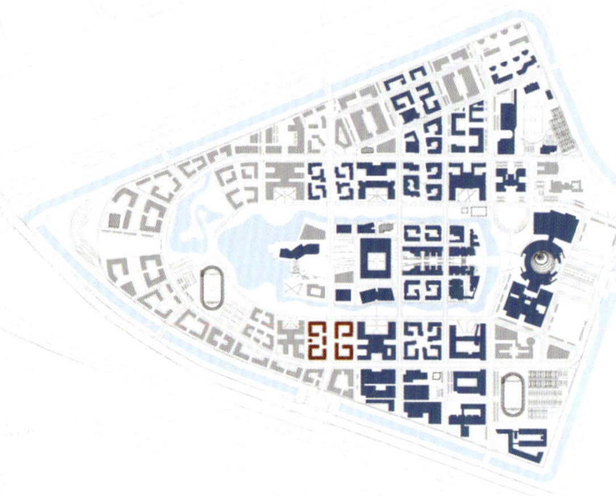

区位图

The Third Student Canteen

第三学生食堂

设计者:周恺、高洪波、陈雍、颜凡明、王力新、郭恩健、王晓宇、安君、曹睿智、刘鑫

Designers: Zhou Kai, Gao Hongpo, Chen Yong, Yan Fanming, Wang Lixin, Guo Enjian, Wang Xiaoyu, An Jun, Cao Ruizhi, Liu Xin

第三学生食堂位于图书馆西北侧地块，北侧为校园景观河流，南侧为开敞绿地，景观条件极佳。主入口面向西侧校园道路，方便师生就餐，东北部设有后勤庭院，后勤出入口位于庭院内，不影响交通和景观，东南侧则设有次入口，面向图书馆来的人流。

考虑到该食堂要有较长的售卖窗口，建筑分为南北两个区，北侧为后厨部分，南侧朝向较好，作为学生就餐区，整个餐厅充满阳光，又能欣赏到南向大面积的绿化景观。两区中间为售卖窗口和排队等候区。为了避免排队和售卖部分采光通风差的不利条件，该区域顶部楼板局部抬高，设置天窗，变消极空间为积极空间。

建筑形体为一简洁的长方体，与图书馆相呼应，并突出图书馆的主体地位。东南两个较长的立面采用凹凸有致的竖向砖垛，通过疏密的变化形成韵律，即体现校园建筑的厚重感，又能通过新的立面语言体现出现代感。砖垛中间为大面积玻璃窗，有利于餐厅的采光与通风。东西立面较短，多为楼梯、卫生间等附属用房，设计采用了水平高带窗，以更好地呼应内部房间的使用功能。

The Third Student Canteen is located in northwest side of the library, with landscape river in the north and open green land in the south, where landscape conditions are excellent. The main entrance faces western campus road, for the convenience of dining of teachers and students. With logistics courtyard in northeast part, logistics entrance is located inside the courtyard, which doesn' t affect transportation and landscape, and the secondary entrance is set in the southeast side, facing people stream form library.

Taking into consideration that the canteen has a long selling window, the building is divided into south and north district. The kitchen is located in the north, while students' dinning area is in the south, so that the restaurant is full of sunlight and students can appreciate greenery landscape. Selling windows and waiting-in-line area are between these two districts. In order to avoid poor lighting and ventilation conditions of selling windows and waiting-in-line area, partial ceiling of such areas are elevated, changing passive space to positive space.

The building is a concise cube, echoing the library and highlighting principal status of the library. Two longer facades in southeast adopt concave-convex vertical piled bricks to form rhythm through density changes, namely embodying decorous feeling of campus building and modern sense through new vertical language. Large-area glass windows are in the middle of piled bricks, which can benefit in favor of restaurant' s lighting and ventilation. The facade of east and west is shorter, where such subsidiary rooms as stairs and toilets, etc. are set, with horizontal windows to echo using function of internal rooms.

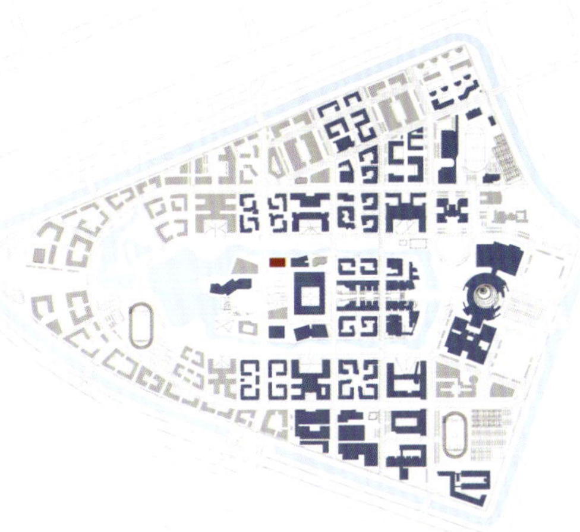

区位图

The Fifth Student Canteen
第五学生食堂

设计者:曲晓舟、张键

Designers: Qu Xiaozhou, Zhang Jian

第五学生食堂用地南侧为景观水系，北侧为图书馆出入口广场，西侧朝向音乐厅，所以设计方案将食堂餐厅布置于用地西侧，三面景观环绕，最大限度利用了用地周边的景观资源。用地东侧紧临新校区第一教学楼山墙，车行道路为尽端式，所以设计将厨房以及厨房后院安排在这一侧，利用教学楼山墙的遮蔽，把厨房对周边环境的影响降至最低。客流主入口设于用地西北侧，紧临有大量人流的西侧道路及广场。客流次入口设于南侧沿景观水系一侧，方便少量散步人流就近进入。厨房后院入口设于东侧尽端路中部，比较隐蔽，也便于车辆掉头。

本设计在有限造价的基础上，着力于功能的合理与优化，并兼顾了外部空间与建筑形象与周边建筑的协调统一。建筑方案立面设计延续了新校区其他已确定方案项目的设计风格，主要饰面材料采用砖红色面砖，并根据总投资情况，减少玻璃幕墙的面积及较大悬挑设计。洞口开窗和体量构成简洁明了而且舒展。由于项目紧临第一教学楼与图书馆，设计方案参考了二者已确定的立面设计，在开窗方面采用了与二者尺度相似的横线条的开口方式，以保证本案与周边建筑的协调和呼应。

Water-landscape system is in the south of the Fifth Student Canteen, library entrance square in the north, and Music Hall in the west, so that canteen restaurant is arranged in the west, surrounded by landscape from three sides, which utilizes surrounding landscape resources maximally. The land is next to the First Teaching Building on the east side and carriage way is dead-end type, so that kitchen and its backyard are arranged in the same side, to reduce effects of kitchen to surroundings to the lowest extent with the use of shield of teaching building. Main entrance is set in the northwest of the land, next to west side road and square. The secondary entrance is set in the south side, for the convenience of access of strolling people. Entrance of kitchen backyard is in the middle of eastern road, secluded and convenient for turning round.

On the basis of limited construction cost, designers focus on rationalization and optimization of functions, which also gives consideration to coordination and unification of outer space and architectural image. Elevation design of building scheme continues design style of other confirmed scheme items of the new campus. Major facing materials are brick-red face bricks, reducing area of glass curtain wall and overhanging design as per total investment situation. Opening windowing and mass construction are concise, bright, and comfortable. The project is next to the First Teaching Building and library, so that its designing scheme refers to the confirmed scheme, to guarantee coordination and echoing of the scheme and surrounding buildings.

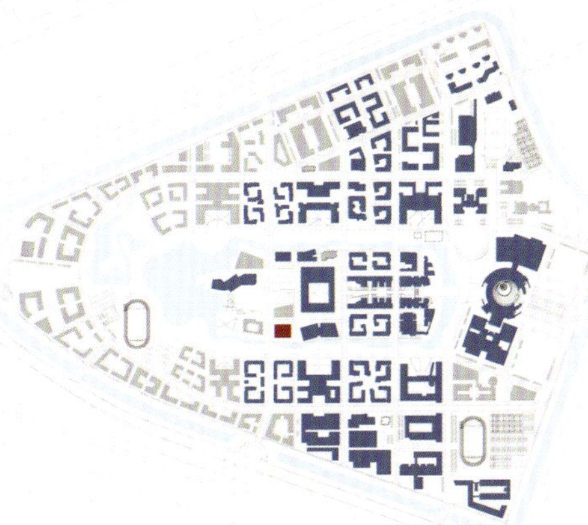

区位图

Smart Campus
智慧校园

老师上课不再需要带U盘等拷贝课件，只需在教室电脑端登录“桌面云系统”即可进入自己的“个人电脑”；智能照明系统根据不同场合、人流量自动调节灯光开关，还可以利用自然光调节室内照度；学生宿舍的电网在“熄灯”后可以识别手机与电脑等不同设备，不允许电脑用电，但却允许学生给手机充电……这是天津大学北洋园新校区向师生们展现出的场景，在云计算、物联网、融合通信、协同办公等信息技术的支撑下，天大新校区将成为一座更加聪明的“智慧校园”。天大新校区的“智慧校园”建设主要体现在以下3个方面。

It is unnecessary for teachers to take U disks for giving a lesson. They can enter into their own “personal computer” through logging in “desk cloud system” in classroom computer desktop; intelligent light system can adjust light switch automatically according to different occasions and visitors flow rate, as well as adjusting indoor illumination with the use of natural light; power grid in students' dormitories can recognize such devices as mobiles and computers after “lights out”, where electricity utilization of computers is not allowed but students can charge mobile phones. The above scenes are shown by Peiyang Garden New Campus of Tianjin University to teachers and students. Supported by such information technologies as cloud computing, internet of things, integrated communication, and cooperative office, the new campus will become a cleverer “smart campus”. Construction of “smart campus” of the new campus is mainly embodied in the following three aspects.

一、以泛在、安全为核心的智慧校园

1、建设泛在的网络系统。新校区以数据中心为大脑，建立包括有线网和全覆盖的无线网在内的智能网络系统，构建了一张遍布校园的智慧网络系统，为师生提供泛在的网络服务。

2、建设校园安全防范系统。将校园各种安防资源统一整合为综合安防管理平台系统，利用最新技术，建设视频监控智能分析系统、防盗报警和紧急求助系统、巡更系统、校园出入口管理系统、校园停车诱导等子系统，为校园安防事件的快速响应和处理、科学分析和决策提供坚实的技术保障。

3、建设消防系统。采用“无线 有线”的组网模式，及时获取校区内各建筑消防设施的运行状况和数据，工作人员在消防指挥中心即可查看现场的设备情况和实时图像，为警情的及时处理提供有力的保障。

4、建设校园信息综合管理平台。结合GIS（地理信息系统）平台建设，建立统一的应急资源数据库、应急值守与指挥系统软件，形成了应急数据中心和决策中心，该中心公共区域和23个分控中心管理的单体建筑的视频图像可实现即时查看和调取，同时进行信息发布。

5、校园导航系统。该系统可以在一幅全校地图上显示所有的教室和实验室信息、运动娱乐场所信息、道路信息、服务机构信息、公寓楼信息、行政办公单位信息等，用户可以方便地查询其功能、所属区域及周边道路等校园导航信息。

I. Smart campus with cores of being ubiquitous and safe

1. Building ubiquitous network system. With the brain of data center, we have built intelligent network system (including wired network and full covered wireless network) and established an intelligent network system spreading all over the campus, so as to provide ubiquitous network services for teachers and students.

2. Building campus security system. Integrate various security resources of the campus into a comprehensive security management platform system and build such sub-systems as video surveillance intelligent analysis system, anti-theft alarm and emergency system, patrol system, campus access management system, and campus parking guidance system, so as to provide solid technical supports for campus security events' quick response and disposal and scientific analysis and decision.

3. Building fire-fighting system. Acquire fire-fighting equipment's running state and data in the campus with the use of "wireless-wired" networking mode. Staffs can look over equipment condition and real-time image in the Fire Command Center, to provide strong guarantee for timely disposal of waning conditions.

4. Building campus information comprehensive management platform. Build unified emergency resource database and emergency duty and command system software with the combination of GIS geographic information system), to form emergency data center and decision center. Video images of the center's public areas and individual buildings of 23 sub-monitor centers can be checked and taken immediately, and publish information at the same time.

5. Building campus navigation system. The system can display all classroom information, lab information, sports and entertainment venues information, road information, facilitating agency information, apartment block information, and administrative office information in a whole-university map, where users can inquire their functions, affiliated regions, and surrounding roads.

二、以高效、便捷为目标的信息校园

1、建设校园一卡通系统。将电子证件应用服务、金融服务、校园商户消费服务、水电控制及场馆计费服务、天津城市一卡通消费服务及门禁管理等功能合并，实现了一张卡解决校园日常生活所需。

2、建设云桌面系统。云桌面系统连接所有电子产品，形成具备无限容量和能力的设备。“桌面云系统”可使每位老师拥有“云端下自己的电脑”，仅这一项技术的运用就将使校内电脑用电比传统方式减少70%以上。

3、建设融合通信系统。融合计算机网络与传统通信网络在同一网络平台，实现IP电话、传真、数据传输、音频会议、呼叫中心、即时通信、视频会议等应用服务。该系统可大大改善我校各教学组团之间、后勤保障部门之间的沟通效率，尤其是突发情况下的应急调度，将在最短时间内得到响应。

4、公共广播系统。校园广播是学校思想政治教育、精神文明建设的重要阵地，校园广播系统替代传统电铃系统，主要用于学校开展教学信息的传播、校园上下课铃声的播放、多媒体校园广播等，具有自动定时播放、预排播放、不同时间播放不同内容、远程广播寻呼等多样化功能。

5、建设多媒体教学系统。多媒体监控中心可监控新校区全部教室，中心的大屏幕显示系统可统一展示各教室上课及考试现场情况；子监考系统覆盖所有70座以上的多媒体教室；多媒体教室均设有投影机、电动幕布、扩声设备、中控台等，扩声系统可实现英语四、六级考试功能；多媒体教学系统采用云边界系统，实现“计算机、媒体终端、中控、网络”四合一功能，接入校承载网，实现新老校区的优质教学资源共享，同时还可实现高清讲课音频和讲义的录制。结合“慕课”的多媒体教学系统建设将使更多学生能在线上点播学习老师的课程，以“远程授课”的形式实现新老校区学生同时上课。

II. Information campus with objectives of being efficient and convenient

1. Building campus card system. Combine electronics certificate application services, financial services, consumption services of campus merchants, water and electricity control and venue charging services, Tianjin city card consumption services, and entrance guard management, to solve daily necessities in the campus with one card.

2. Building cloud desktop system. Cloud desktop system connects all electronic products to form the device with infinite capacity and ability. Each teacher can possess "their own computers under the cloud" with "desktop cloud system", so that electricity utilization of computers in the campus can be saved by above 70%.

3. Building converged communication system. Integrate computer network and traditional communication network in the same network platform, to realize such application services as IP phone, fax, data transmission, audio conference, call center, instant messaging, and video conference. The system can largely improve communication efficiency among teaching groups and logistics departments, particularly emergency dispatch under emergencies.

4. Building public address system. Campus broadcast is an important position of the university' s ideological and political education and spiritual civilization. Replacing traditional bell system, campus broadcast system is mainly used for spreading the university' s teaching information, and playing class attending and finishing bell and multimedia campus broadcast, which can play at fixed time automatically, conduct beforehand arrangement, and play different contents at different time.

5. Building multimedia teaching system. Multimedia supervision center can supervise all classrooms of the new campus, while large screen display system in the center can show class and exam conditions of each classroom; sub invigilating system is covered in all multimedia classrooms of above 70 seats; all multimedia classrooms are equipped with projectors, power-driven curtains, amplified sound devices, and center consoles, and sound-reinforcement system can realize CET-4 and CET-6 exams; multimedia teaching system adopts cloud boundary system to realize the four-in-one function, namely "computer, media terminal, center control, and network", to realize share of excellent teaching resources of new campus and old campus and to record high-definition audios and videos. With "MOOCS" multimedia teaching system, more students can play and learn teachers' lessons on the internet, to realize having class jointly in the way of "remote teaching"

三、以“低碳、节能”为主题的绿色校园

天津大学新校区的建设目标是“绿色、生态、节约型校园”。传统校园由于集体用水和电的方式，使在校大学生人均耗能量是城镇居民的数倍。天津大学能源监测系统采用物联网、云计算、精细计量、数字传感等先进技术，能够实时、全面、准确地采集水、电、气、热等各种能耗数据，对能耗数据集中进行详细的分类和统计分析，形成各个监测单元的年度、月度、每日、每小时乃至每分钟的能耗曲线，生成详细的数据报表。根据分析结果采取相应的节能管理措施，通过管理节能、行为节能、科技节能相结合共同达到节约能耗的目的。

III. Green campus with the theme of "low-carbon and energy conservation"

The construction target of the new campus of Tianjin University is "green, ecological, and conservation-oriented campus". Average energy consumption of college students is several times of that of urban residents for collective water and electricity utilization. With the use of such advanced technologies as internet of things, cloud computing, elaborative measuring, and digital sensor, Energy Supervisor System of Tianjin University can collect various energy consumption data (such as water, electricity, gas, and heating) in real time, completely and accurately, which forms yearly, monthly, daily, hourly, and minutely energy consumption curve and detailed data statement through classifying and analyzing energy consumption data. Take corresponding energy-saving management measures according to analysis results. Save energy in management, behaviors, and science and technology.

后记

天津大学北洋园校区的建设，承载了所有天大人的梦想。新校区从2009年开始筹建，到2011年全面开工建设，再到2015年9月全面投用，生机勃勃地、以全新的姿态迎接师生、校友及120年校庆日的到来，在从无到有的校园建设过程中，凝聚了无数人的心血和智慧。

北洋园校区建设是天津大学发展史上的一件大事，关系到天津大学的长远发展，是我们承担的重大的历史重担。为纪念这一历史事件，并让所有关心天大发展的师生、校友、各界人士全面了解新校区的方方面面，特编纂此书。

本书从2015年1月开始策划以来，得到校领导、相关部门的全力帮助和支持。120年校庆筹备办公室、校友总会、建筑学院为本书从内容组织，到装帧形式都给予了详尽的指导意见。新校区规划建设管理办公室在百忙之中，仔细梳理了新校区建设的所有信息，提供了新校区规划建设概况、历程、智慧校园的详尽内容，有助于读者对新校区的全面了解。天津大学党委宣传部提供了新校区113处道路、景观、楼宇等的命名来源，有效体现新老校区的文化传承和历史传承。所有工作营的设计大师和杰出校友，在席不暇暖的设计工作中，仍抽出宝贵时间整理提供了新校区总体规划、景观规划和22组单体建筑详细准确的图文资料，以期能在书中使读者了解建筑背后更深一层的设计立意。

最后，籍以此书，感谢你们。

感谢你们，新校区建设的筹建者和指导者，你们的远见卓识、统筹兼顾、有力推进，使天大的发展有了更广阔的平台。

感谢你们，始终坚持在一线的天津大学的建设者们，6个春去冬来、寒来暑往，你们为新校区的建设栉风沐雨、呕心沥血，从各个方面全力保障新校区建设达到最理想目标。

感谢你们，参与新校区规划设计的建筑大师、校友们，你们以新校区建设为己任，案牍劳形、匠心独运，为新校区富有意蕴的美丽容颜而殚精竭虑。

感谢你们，各个参与新校区建设的建工集团，来自施工、监理、检测等单位的数千名施工人员，在看见的、看不见的区域，在新校区的各个工地上，不管是赤阳炎炎的夏日，还是朔风凛冽的寒冬，始终奋战在建设第一线。

感谢你们，天津大学的所有师生和海内外校友，你们的关心与支持，永远是学校不断发展的动力。

“圆梦新校区，启航新甲子”，祝愿天津大学在新老校区的土地上，同时开启新甲子，扬帆远航，圆兴国强学之梦。

Postscript

The construction of Peiyang Garden Campus of Tianjin University bears the dreams of all people in Tianjin University. The new campus was prepared for construction in 2009, which started for construction completely in 2011, and put into use in September, 2015. It welcomes teachers, students, alumni, and 120th which anniversary lively. During campus construction, painstaking efforts and wisdom of countless people are gathered.

The construction of the new campus is an event in the development history of Tianjin University, touching on long-term development of Tianjin University, which is a great historical burden we shall take. We hereby compile the book to memorize the historical event and to make all teachers, students, alumni, and people from all walks of life concerning development of Tianjin University know about every aspect of the new campus.

University leaders and relevant departments have spared no efforts in helping and supporting the book since its planning in January, 2015. 120th Anniversary Preparatory Office, General Assembly of Alumni, and School of Architecture have given detailed guiding ideas to the book from content organization to binding layout. New Campus Planning and Construction Management Office has taken the time out to do up all information of new campus construction and provided detailed contents in new campus' planning and construction conditions, course, and smart campus, which contribute to know about the new campus comprehensively. Party Committee Propaganda Department of Tianjin University has offered name sources of 113 roads, landscapes, and buildings, embodying cultural inheritance and historical inheritance of the new and old campus. Designers have spared the time to offer detailed and accurate graphic files of the new campus' overall planning, landscape planning, and 22 groups of individual buildings, so that readers can know about deeper design conceptions of buildings.

At last, we hereby thank you in the book.

Thank you, preparation personnel and conductors for construction of the new campus, for making Tianjin University' s development have wider platform, with your foresight, full consideration, and powerful boost.

Thank you, constructors insisting in the construction front line of Tianjin University, for devoting to constructing the new campus in the past six years, to guarantee construction of the new campus from all aspects.

Thank you, master architects and alumni participating in planning and design of the new campus, for taking great cares to construct the new campus beautifully.

Thank you, construction engineering groups participating in construction of the new campus and thousands of constructors from construction units, supervising units, and detection units, for constructing at every construction site, in burning hot summer or brutal winter.

Thank you, all teachers and students of Tianjin University and alumni at home and abroad, for concerning and supporting Tianjin University.

"Fullfill Dreams of New Campus, Beginning a New 60-year Circle" . Wish that Tianjin University can realize the dream of rejuvenating the country in the new and old campus.

图书在版编目（CIP）数据

圆梦新校区 启航新甲子：天津大学北洋园新校区规划建设实录 /
《圆梦新校区 启航新甲子：天津大学北洋园新校区规划建设实录》编委会著.
— 天津：天津大学出版社，2015.8
（北洋文库）
ISBN 978-7-5618-5408-2

Ⅰ. ①圆… Ⅱ. ①圆… Ⅲ. ①高等学校－建筑设计－天津市 Ⅳ. ①TU244.3

中国版本图书馆CIP数据核字(2015)第209856号

责任编辑：朱玉红
美术编辑：盖 群 贺诗淇 岳意贺
全书策划：天大乙未文化工作室
编辑邮箱：yiweiculture@126.com

出版发行 天津大学出版社
地　　址 天津市卫津路92号天津大学内（邮编：300072）
电　　话 发行部 022-27403647
网　　址 publish.tju.edu.cn
印　　刷 北京华联印刷有限公司
经　　销 全国各地新华书店
开　　本 210mm×285mm
印　　张 18
字　　数 210千
版　　次 2015年9月第1版
印　　次 2015年9月第1次
定　　价 298.00元